CRACKS IN THE
CONSENSUS

THE WASHINGTON PAPERS

. . . intended to meet the need for an authoritative, yet prompt, public appraisal of the major developments in world affairs.

President, CSIS: David M. Abshire

Series Editor: Walter Laqueur

Director of Studies: Erik R. Peterson

Director of Publications: James R. Dunton

Managing Editor: Donna R. Spitler

MANUSCRIPT SUBMISSION

The Washington Papers and Praeger Publishers welcome inquiries concerning manuscript submissions. Please include with your inquiry a curriculum vitae, synopsis, table of contents, and estimated manuscript length. Manuscript length must fall between 30,000 and 45,000 words. All submissions will be peer reviewed. Submissions to *The Washington Papers* should be sent to *The Washington Papers*; The Center for Strategic and International Studies; 1800 K Street NW; Suite 400; Washington, DC 20006. Book proposals should be sent to Praeger Publishers; 88 Post Road West; P.O. Box 5007; Westport, CT 06881-5007.

The Washington Papers/172

CRACKS IN THE CONSENSUS

Debating the Democracy Agenda in U.S. Foreign Policy

Howard J. Wiarda

Foreword by
Georges A. Fauriol

PUBLISHED WITH
THE CENTER FOR STRATEGIC
AND INTERNATIONAL STUDIES

Westport, Connecticut
London

Library of Congress Cataloging-in-Publication Data

Wiarda, Howard J., 1939–
  Cracks in the consensus : debating the democracy agenda in U.S.
foreign policy / Howard J. Wiarda.
      p.   cm. – (The Washington papers ; 172)
    "Published with the Center for Strategic and International
Studies."
    Includes bibliographical references and index.
    ISBN 0-275-96101-X (cloth : alk. paper). – ISBN 0-275-96100-1
(paper : alk. paper)
      1. United States–Foreign relations–20th century–Case studies.
  2. Democracy–History–20th century.   I. Title.   II. Series.
  E744.W542   1997
  327.73–dc21   97-15579

British Library Cataloguing in Publication data is available.

Library of Congress Catalog Card Number: 97-15579
ISBN: 0-275-96101-X (cloth)
        0-275-96100-1 (paper)

First published in 1997

Praeger Publishers, 88 Post Road West, Westport, CT 06881
An imprint of Greenwood Publishing Group, Inc.

Printed in the United States of America

∞™

The paper used in this book complies with the Permanent
Paper Standard issued by the National Information Standards
Organization (Z39.48-1984).

10   9   8   7   6   5   4   3   2   1

Contents

Foreword

Modern democracies demand time-consuming calibration. Their individual parts – citizens, material resources – require careful assembly and, if history is any judge, in many cases generate messy outcomes. Essentially unstructured and free-flowing, democracies ultimately become functional only because of institutions that are able to modulate the varying competing pressures in society. It is in the fine tuning of those institutions that democracies of the late twentieth century have become an extraordinary machinery of political and economic management.

That remarkable achievement is of a recent vintage – a 200 year record, more or less, with democratic governance acquiring a truly universal charter only in the last 50. Arguably, even this time frame may be somewhat exaggerated, but is made possible by the victorious outcome of Western democracies over Soviet-sponsored totalitarianism. The hallmark of democracy is hardly efficiency – flexibility is a much more descriptive term. Democracy's success at the dawn of the twenty-first century is made possible by its strategic marriage to free market capitalism. This combination generates an imperfect but vibrant bazaar of ideas – a marketplace of resources whose interaction is in effect self-regulated through citizen institutions and, ultimately, freely elected government.

The highly evolved characteristics of democratic governance in the late 1990s may point to a nearly exclusive and universal claim on political management. There is an endearing quality to this notion of the "end of history." However, the terms of reference for policymakers and citizens are more ambivalent. In many ways the democratic record is defining itself around the world on the basis of varied political and economic experiences, some of which may diverge in their specificity from the North Atlantic historical context. The point here is not so much that there are different forms of democracy but that its achievement can be a disorienting zigzag.

These are major challenges for policymakers and scholars alike. Articulating visions of democracy, let alone promoting them in the context of foreign policy, does not always graduate beyond rhetoric. Operationalizing these visions is an even greater hurdle.

This novel study by Howard Wiarda addresses such issues. Directed particularly at U.S. policymakers, this effort reflects Dr. Wiarda's command of both U.S. foreign policy and political development analyses. He provides a timely overview of the democratic experience in key regions of the world, backed up with helpful case studies of the Latin American and Caribbean area. At issue is the effectiveness of U.S. democratization policy and the lessons learned. The author's conclusions—democracy is not irreversible and U.S. policy toward it is far from being infallible—may be a timely wake-up call.

The challenge Dr. Wiarda poses is anchored by three themes: first, that democracy means different things to different people; second, that democratic successes are shaped by factors difficult to reorient in the short term, such as a nation's historical trials and tribulation; and third, that U.S. policy instruments and ethnocentric interests do not always couple well with U.S. national interests. Wiarda sets out seven timely policy guidelines to reconcile these three themes. Readers may not share all of his analyses and conclusions, but they are at least likely to think through more carefully their own assumptions.

Georges A. Fauriol
Director
Americas Program, CSIS

June 1997

Preface

Americans have now largely exhausted the old debate about democracy and human rights versus realism and the national interest in U.S. foreign policy. Most now agree that the democracy/human rights agenda is not just an expression of American idealism but constitutes an important and quite hard-headed instrument of U.S. foreign policy; at the same time, we recognize that in pursuing a policy of national interest, democracy and human rights are important components—at least in America—in that formula. The old ideological quarrels between idealists and realists still surface from time to time, especially regarding President Clinton's foreign policy; but much of the debate—and this monograph—now centers on the balance between these two, the relative weight to assign to each, how to achieve *both* democracy and other (economic, diplomatic, strategic) foreign policy goals.

Indeed, since the 1980s and the end of the Cold War, a quite remarkable, bipartisan consensus has emerged in U.S. foreign policy centered on three main pillars: democracy (including human rights), free trade (including regional trade pacts), and open markets. The Mexican *peso* crisis of 1994 shook but did not topple the consensus on free trade and open markets; but now events in Poland (electoral victory by former communists), Bosnia (limited implementation of the Dayton Peace Accords), Russia (ongoing challenges to democracy), Mexico (potential instability with immense repercussions for U.S. society and domestic politics), and other recent, crisis-prone elections and electoral outcomes force us to rethink at a deeper level the implications of the democracy agenda. For in some countries U.S. policy is damaging democracy rather than strengthening it, undermining stability, and inadvertently destabilizing countries that we can ill afford to see destabilized.

The issue is complicated by the bureaucratic difficulty in Washington, D.C., of fashioning a consensus on *any* foreign policy strategy, including the democracy agenda. Once established with all the attendant compromises and accommodations, thereafter it becomes very difficult to reopen and reexamine the various elements of the consensus all over again. There is an understandable reluctance to reconsider issues that had seemingly been settled, to reopen a topic whose earlier resolution had taken so much inter-and intra-agency time and effort. Yet reexamination is necessary if policy is to remain both forward-looking and realistic.

The issue is further complicated by both the moralistic history and tone of U.S. foreign policy, and by the institutional apparatus already in place to advance the democracy agenda. The United States has long had a missionary aspect to its foreign policy; Americans want to do "good" in the world; we want to pursue not only our national interests but, à la Woodrow Wilson, to bring the benefits of our civilization (politically, economically, morally) to the "less-favored" or "developing" nations. At the same time, these are no longer just abstract intellectual arguments but are backed by both private human rights and pro-democracy groups and public agencies within the State Department, the Agency for International Development, et cetera, and large-scale lobbying efforts dedicated to advancing democracy. The purpose here is not to quarrel with the recent consensus on foreign policy, including democracy, or with the moral basis of U.S. foreign policy, because this volume supports these goals. But it is necessary to point out some of the practical problems and pitfalls of a democracy-based foreign policy, to offer a conceptual apparatus for addressing the complex issues involved, and to suggest how policy can be improved.

The problems with the democracy agenda are several: here

we only introduce the main issues while discussing them in detail in the body of the study. First, the democracy agenda was largely conceived during the Cold War (Poland, Russia, El Salvador) as a way of demonstrating that our system was better than the Soviets' or of stabilizing unstable countries; but now that the Cold War has ended, the goals and purposes of the program need to be rethought. Second, U.S. policymakers tend, for understandable political purposes, to proclaim a country "democratic" (Haiti) when in fact it is only part-way there; such claims often do a disservice to the country affected by raising unrealistic expectations for it, and they may force U.S. policy into a straightjacket that rules out nuance and flexibility. Third, there are numerous, continuing, practical problems in a pro-democracy foreign policy: how much pressure to bring to bear, with what instruments, how to balance off democracy against other U.S. interests, whether to allow exceptions (China, Vietnam, Saudi Arabia, Kuwait, Egypt, Algeria), and how many.

Nor should Americans forget, fourth, that democracy is not a cure-all, that democracy and free markets often cause a new set of ongoing problems that demand continuing U.S. policy attention. Fifth is the problem of dealing with forms and meanings of "democracy" other than our own, some of which are not very democratic. A related problem, sixth, is the tendency to see democracy as an either-or proposition rather than as a continuum, an ongoing process; we need to recognize both distinct *types* as well as *degrees* of democracy. Seventh, we need to raise the very real possibility that U.S. efforts on behalf of democracy may have the unintended effect of destabilizing some countries (Mexico, possibly Russia) whom we should least wish to see destabilized.

The real world is of course far more complicated, and interesting, than that encompassed in the dictatorship-democracy dichotomy. Not only are there distinct meanings of democracy (Anglo-American, French, Asian, Latin American, et cetera), but there are also many gradations, including partial democracy, guided democracy, delegated democracy—democracy with a great variety of adjectives. Americans lack the conceptual categories to understand the many "halfway houses" and "crazy-quilt patterns" of democracy, and we often lack the policy sophistication to address appropriately the mixed and varied forms of democracy that we frequently encounter in the real world.

It is this conceptual armature that this volume seeks to provide. It goes beyond earlier criticisms by suggesting concrete policy steps that need to be taken. The study contains both general discussion as well as case study materials. It begins with a general overview of the democracy agenda in U.S. foreign policy: the history of the "Wilsonian impulse" (teaching other countries to "elect good men") in foreign policy, past debates over the issue of having democracy at the core of foreign policy, the emergence of the recent consensus on the democracy agenda, the questions that continue to swirl around the policy, and how the end of the Cold War forces us to reformulate the policy. The introductory chapter also explores the diverse meanings of democracy; the degrees, types, and gradations of democracy; and the clash between universal democratic norms and more particular, country- or region-specific ways of doing things. This chapter frames the debate, raises the issues, and emphasizes the important policy implications.

The next two chapters provide case study materials. In chapter 2 examples are drawn from diverse but crucially important global regions: Russia, East Asia, Eastern Europe, the Islamic world, and Africa. In chapter 3, dealing with Latin America, the focus narrows to countries of major importance to the United States but whose democracies remain unconsolidated: Mexico, Haiti, Peru, Guatemala, Venezuela, the Dominican Republic. These case study chapters are not meant to be definitive or complete assessments of political conditions in these areas or countries but to concentrate more specifically on the diverse definitions and types of democracy, the fact that democracy exists in various gradations and mixed forms, the policy dilemmas involved, and the need for the United States to develop a more sophisticated understanding of the diverse institutional arrangements within the universe of democracy.

The final chapter, building on the earlier theoretical discussion as well as the case study materials, explores the policy implications and offers solutions. How can the United States both stand for democracy and its advancement while also recognizing the diverse meanings and understandings of that term? How can Americans promote democracy without that becoming potentially a self-defeating moral crusade? How can we advance democracy without running unacceptable risks of destabilizing the very countries we are seeking to assist? How do we reconcile, as in China, Saudi Arabia, or Algeria, democracy goals with other important policy objectives? In fact, policymakers at a pragmatic level are often adept at reaching decisions on regimes that fall short of full-scale democracy, but such compromises often evoke recriminations and partisan debate. This study seeks to resolve the issues associated with the democracy debate while also suggesting to policymakers a set of conceptual categories and a framework to deal with regimes that are often only partially democratic but with whom we must nevertheless have good relations, at the same time offering possibilities to these countries to take the next step *toward* democracy.

This monograph was prepared while I was a senior associate of the Center for Strategic and International Studies (CSIS) in Washington, D.C. My colleagues in the Americas Program there—Georges Fauriol, director; Sidney Weintraub, Delal Baer, Joyce Hoebing, Christopher Sands, Lowell Fleischer, Armand Peschard-Sverdrup—warmly encouraged this and other research projects and offered a particularly hospitable and dynamic working atmosphere for observing and being a part of the Washington "policy loop." This research has also benefitted from my window on policy at the National War College, 1991–1996, and from the support of my "home" institution over the years, the University of Massachusetts/Amherst and especially its Department of Political Science. Doris Holden skillfully typed the manuscript and Thomas Carothers, Georges Fauriol, and Sidney Weintraub read and commented on it. Donna Spitler and James Dunton of CSIS's Publications Department performed creative editorial work. The author alone, however, is responsible for the analysis and interpretation.

Howard J. Wiarda
Washington, D.C

June 1997

xiii

CRACKS IN THE CONSENSUS

1

The Democracy Agenda in U.S. Foreign Policy

American Exceptionalism

The United States has long proclaimed that it is "different" from other nations, both in domestic politics and in foreign affairs. In domestic politics, stretching back to the founding of the republic, America has stood for life, liberty, equality, and, as the Declaration of Independence puts it, the "pursuit of happiness." American politics has, over the centuries, tended toward greater democracy, openness, pluralism, and transparency. America has long believed in limited government, a weak state, checks and balances, and, as John Locke, the founding oracle of Anglo-American republicanism put it, "estate," by which he meant the right to acquire, hold, and dispose of private property. In all these ways, America sought to set itself apart from the Old World of European nations, which did not regularly practice these traits and from which most of the early colonists in America had come.[1]

But right from the beginning America believed in and practiced exceptionalism in its foreign affairs as well as in its domestic politics and beliefs. In the famous doctrine that bears his name, President James Monroe compared the Old World of European powers with the New World of the Americas. *They* are mainly monarchies and practitioners of absolutism and autocracy, he said, while *we* practice republicanism. *They* believe in domination and tyranny while *we* practice liberty. Moreover, *they* practice the European strategies of colonization and empire while *we* believe in freedom. And *they* utilize the Old World techniques of diplomatic secrecy, balance of power, and Machiavellianism while *we* are the apostles of openness, moral precepts, and honor. These contrasts between Old World practices *and* the stated goals of the new United States could not have been portrayed more starkly.

Moreover, in the actual *conduct* of its foreign affairs the United States continued to practice and proclaim its distinctiveness—even while later skeptics expressed doubts as to the purity of American motives. For example, in the wars of Texas independence (1836) and with Mexico (1846), when the United States deprived Mexico of roughly 40 percent of its national territory, the United States justified its land and power grabs with the nobler language of "manifest destiny," "self-determination," and "Westward expansionism"—to say nothing of anti-Mexican, anti-Spanish, anti-Catholic racism, xenophobia, and prejudice.

When the United States defeated Spain in the war of 1898 and seized Puerto Rico and the Philippines while establishing a protectorate over Cuba, there is no doubt the American public believed it was operating morally in behalf of the peoples affected, not just in self-interest. When the United States "stole" (Teddy Roosevelt's words) Panama from Colombia in 1902 in order to build the Canal, and subsequently sent military occupation forces to Cuba, the Dominican Republic, Haiti, Nicaragua, and Panama, no one can question that Americans genuinely *thought* they were bringing the benefits of a superior civilization (democracy, elections, Protestantism, free enterprise) to "less fortunate" lands and peoples.

America has thus always justified its great power or national interest pursuits with the *language* of moral superiority and purpose. The need for high moral purpose both reflects American beliefs and reinforces the sense of American distinctiveness from other powers who practice *realpolitik*. This need for high moral purpose in U.S. foreign policy extends to today: when George Bush sent U.S. troops to the Persian Gulf in 1991 to defend U.S.

oil interests, it was not sufficient for him to proclaim that the United States was operating from the principle of self-interest. Instead, he had to demonize Saddam Hussein as a new Hitler and proclaim U.S. military efforts to roll back the Iraqi forces as a war against "naked aggression." Similarly, current U.S. efforts in China or Russia cannot be set forth as simply balance-of-power politics or the effort to check and contain former or future rivals and adversaries but as a campaign to bring democracy, free enterprise, and human rights to these nations.

In most cases throughout history—such as World Wars I and II—American statements of moral purpose and the pursuit of hard-headed national interests went hand-in-hand. That is, the United States went to war against Germany and the Axis powers both to defend threatened U.S. interests globally and in Europe, as well as to "make the world safe for democracy" or to defeat fascism. The Cold War for all those decades was both a strategy to contain the Soviet Union and to defeat "Godless communism." In these cases there was generally little contradiction between morality and self-interest and hence comparatively few problems in the conduct of U.S. policy. But occasionally, as in Vietnam, and perhaps more recently in Haiti, Somalia, and Bosnia, U.S. moral rhetoric and national interest goals seem not in harmony. Or the facts on the ground belie the rhetoric, which then proves hollow. Or the United States begins taking literally or too seriously the moral goals, elevating them to a vaunted position above its national interest goals. Policy often becomes a prisoner of and paralyzed by our own rhetoric. It is then that U.S. foreign policy gets in trouble, for ends and means do not match up, the goals come to appear unreachable and unrealistic, and the public, the Congress, and the media stop supporting the policy.

This study contends that, with the newest expression of American high moral purpose, the democracy agenda, the United States is currently verging on such a disjuncture. The lofty goals of the policy and the limited means Americans are willing to use to achieve it appear at times to be out of balance. The rhetoric and ideology of the democracy agenda have come to overshadow the national interest concerns involved. Even worse, the strategy seems not consistently to be producing friendly, stable regimes but too often results in the opposite consequences. The results, for example, of recent democracy efforts and the election strategy in such diverse areas as Haiti, Mexico, Algeria, Pakistan, Russia, and Bosnia may be to produce instability rather than stability, chaos rather than order, national breakdowns deleterious to U.S. interests instead of happy, peaceful, friendly, democratic regimes.

At the least, the issue merits serious review and reconsideration. I should say that I myself am a strong believer in democracy and human rights as a part of U.S. foreign policy–both because they conform to my own beliefs and because I do not believe it is possible to have an effective *American* foreign policy unless it can be justified on moral and idealistic grounds. But to be successful the policy needs to be carried out effectively, the moral and self-interest motives need to be kept in accord, and the policy needs to produce concrete, positive results that the public can see and appreciate. Because these features I believe are now out of kilter, this volume explores the dimensions of the problem and suggests new solutions.

The Democracy Agenda

The democracy agenda suggests that the pursuit of democracy and human rights is and ought to be at the heart of U.S. foreign policy purpose. Almost no one disagrees with that focus anymore. Even such hard-headed apostles of *realpolitik* as George Kennan and Henry Kissinger, who in the past criticized America's moralistic crusades in foreign policy and called for a policy based exclusively on national interest considerations, now recognize that for an *American* (as distinct from those still Machiavellian Europeans) foreign policy to be successful, it must have a strong democracy/human rights component to it. If the policy lacks this moral dimension, then the public, Congress, religious and human rights groups, labor unions, and even, now, the foreign policy establishment is unlikely to support it, and the policy probably cannot succeed.[2]

But if there is a consensus by now on the need for a democracy/human rights component to U.S. foreign policy, that still leaves open the question of how strong that component should be. Should it be the only or clearly the most important element in our foreign policy, or should it be but one consideration among several? Therein lies the current rub—and the policy conflict. For while almost no one disagrees anymore that democracy and human rights should form *some part* of the foreign policy agenda, the question remains as to the degree, the relative importance of the democracy component, as compared with other considerations.

A few preliminary comments and distinctions will help frame the debate. First, although most of us want a democracy/human rights component in U.S. foreign policy, we also accept the maxim that no rule needs to be 100 percent pure in order to serve as an effective basis for policy. For example, other than an occasional embassy *démarche* on the national palace, Americans do not talk very much about democracy and human rights in such countries as Kuwait and Saudi Arabia. The reason is obvious: although we would obviously prefer democracy in these two countries, our and the rest of the world's (Japan as well as Western Europe) absolute dependence on Persian Gulf oil for the health of our national economies means that in practice we have opted to largely ignore the democracy-advancing aspects of our policy in favor of a stable (we hope) but nondemocratic regime that provides us with a reliable source of oil. There are relatively few dissents from this policy; we do not proclaim it publicly but informally almost everyone agrees that U.S. prosperity and the health of our economy and jobs—all of which depend on Middle East oil—are simply more important in these two cases than a too vigorous and potentially destabilizing democracy/human rights policy.

National security issues are approached similarly. Because of the long Cold War with the Soviet Union and the threat posed by Soviet armaments and missiles, the strategic dimensions of that relationship took overwhelming precedence over democracy or any other dimension. The defense of U.S. security and the threat posed by the Soviets was *the* number one priority; all other considerations were secondary, for without national security, it was argued, there could be neither democracy nor human rights. Moreover, as with the oil issue in Kuwait or Saudi Arabia, few questioned the ultimate priority of the security relationship vis-à-vis the Soviet Union.

Questions arose mainly on the periphery where, in fact, some of the most intense Cold War battles were fought out: Southeast Asia, the Middle East, Sub-Saharan Africa, Central America. There the issue was often joined as to whether the Cold War security issues ought to take priority or whether local conditions of poverty, human rights abuses, and *lack* of democracy had caused the problems. In general, however, as long as the Cold War was being waged in all its intensity, whenever the security aspects of U.S. policy conflicted with the "softer" or pro-democracy facets, the security considerations won out. The policy became known in the 1960s and 1970s as the "lesser evil doctrine": when faced with a choice between a strong autocrat who is anti-communist and protects our interests (Marcos, the Shah, Diem, Sukarno, Batista, Trujillo, other military-authoritarian regimes) *and* a wobbly democrat who may coddle the Left and prove unstable, the United States would almost always opt for the lesser evil of the stable autocrat.[3]

But now let us introduce some complications into what has been a fairly clear-cut case:

1. The United States discovered in the Cuba case that supposedly stable authoritarians like Batista, rather than preserving stability and anti-communism, may actually prepare the ground in which radical revolutions like Castro's may flourish. This dawning realization prompted a reevaluation of U.S. policy toward Trujillo, Marcos, Diem, Somoza, and others.

2. The United States began to realize in the early 1980s, following Jimmy Carter's earlier romantic and idealistic policy of human rights that was often self-defeating, that a hard-headed democracy/human rights agenda could be used as a way of destabilizing the Soviet Union and the Warsaw Pact countries. In other words, instead of the perpetual conflict between strategic

and human rights considerations in foreign policy, the Reagan administration sought to utilize democracy and human rights as a strategic weapon to weaken, delegitimize, and undermine the Soviets and their allies.[4]

3. Similarly in El Salvador in the early 1980s—and then in many other countries—U.S. human rights policy acquired a practical as well as an idealistic dimension. Instead of being hammered for its focus on the strategic as opposed to the democracy, human rights, and socioeconomic dimensions of the several Central American conflicts, the administration discovered that by standing for democracy and human rights it could defuse the critics in Congress, the media, and the religious and human rights groups, provide internal bureaucratic unity to its policy, get otherwise critical allies to support the policy, secure a more centrist government in El Salvador (as distinct from the unhappy choice between a rapacious military and a guerrilla triumph), and actually carry out its security strategy more effectively. The positive benefits from the El Salvador experience served as a model for similar strategies elsewhere in Latin America, Asia, Eastern Europe, and eventually the Soviet Union.[5]

4. In general, the arguments between advocates of the primacy of the strategic dimension in U.S. foreign policy and the advocates of other dimensions have been largely static and dichotomous: either one or the other. But in the recent debate over China policy a more dynamic dimension has been added: that emphasis on the trade and economic side of the relationship would, in the long run, improve both human rights and the strategic relationship. The issue was the renewal of Most Favored Nation (MFN) status to China. Human rights groups opposed the measure on the grounds it would be rewarding China for its various human rights abuses, mainly the crushing of the student democracy movement in Tiananmen Square. But business groups wanting to trade with China argued that the economic growth generated would improve living standards and the human rights situation in the long term, and would also serve to anchor a more prosperous China as a stable and responsible international participant in the world economy. In this way, instead of the usual

conflict and zero-sum trade-off between democracy/human rights and trade/strategic considerations, the latter was pictured in a dynamic and positive relationship to the former.

5. The end of the Cold War has altered all these givens—including in the China case above. With the disintegration of the Soviet Union and the Warsaw Pact, and with no powerful strategic threat looming immediately on the horizon, the United States can now pay more serious attention to democracy/human rights concerns, and less to strategic issues, than in the past. The equation or trade-off, always delicately balanced, between the democracy/human rights agenda and the strategic one has now been tipped definitely toward the former. China provides an example—which is what made the ongoing debate over MFN so close. As long as the Cold War was still on, the United States needed to use China in a strategic sense ("the China card") to counterbalance and play off against the Soviets. But with the Cold War over, the United States no longer so strongly needs China's strategic presence on the Soviet border and can afford to emphasize human rights issues more than in the past.

6. One further new factor merits an introductory mention here—the growth of pro-democracy/human rights lobbying groups and of a "cottage industry" of organizations, both private and public, aimed at furthering the democracy/human rights agenda. When the human rights issue first came up as a major issue in foreign policy in the early 1970s, there were few human rights lobbies; but now there are a *host* of general and specialized religious and human rights groups, foundations, and constituencies dedicated to advancing that agenda. In addition, we now have the National Endowment for Democracy (NED), the Democratic and Republican international affairs institutes, agencies for democracy and human rights in the Agency for International Development (AID), the State Department, and the White House, and again a variety of public, private, and public-private election observer agencies (such as the Carter Center). In other words, the debate between the strategic and the democracy/human rights aspects of policy is no longer just a "rational-choice" process among policymaking elites of carefully weighing alternatives and options; rather, it is now the "stuff" of intense lobbying,

street (and church, synagogue, town meeting, etc.) activity, pressure politics, congressional interest and posturing, partisan disagreement, and significant bureaucratic interests and rivalries. These activities have also forced a change over the past 20 years in the strategic-democracy/human rights equation.

The Wilsonian Tradition in Foreign Policy

We often speak of democracy and human rights as if these were new (the past 20 years) items on the U.S. foreign policy agenda. But in fact, the United States has long had this moralistic, idealistic strain as part of its foreign policy. Indeed, one could say that the United States, founded on the ideals of liberty and freedom, has *always* had these elements as part of its foreign policy. As Jeane Kirkpatrick once remarked to the author, "What are we as a nation if we do not stand for democracy and human rights?"

Of course, motives are almost always mixed, and diplomatic history is full of examples where U.S. territorial or power grabs were covered over with the language of high-sounding principles. Or, where moralism and self-interest overlapped and got mixed together. Nevertheless, there is—perhaps unique among nations: "American exceptionalism" again—a strong streak of wanting to do good in the world, as distinct from naked self-interest. Even the fact that America feels compelled to justify its power politics by the use of moralistic argument—and then often becomes a prisoner of its own rhetoric—is itself an indicator of the importance of idealism in policy.

When the Monroe Doctrine was promulgated in 1823 at the height of the Latin American independence movements, there is no doubt that most Americans favored the cause of the new republics—even while Henry Clay cautioned a national interest strategy of wait-and-see. When Andrew Jackson acquired Florida from Spain, and then subsequently when the United States took Texas and the Southwest from Mexico, there is no doubt most Americans believed these territories would be better off, better blessed, and more productive under American than Mexican rule. And who can doubt the sincerity of William McKinley who allegedly prayed for divine guidance the night before seizing the Philippines?

Similarly with Panama in 1902: we may have nefariously "stolen" Panama from Colombia but at least we did so, in former Senator Hayakawa's immortal words, "fair and square." When Woodrow Wilson sent U.S. Marines to occupy a half dozen countries in Central America and the Caribbean, he and others doubtless believed they could "teach" the Latins to use the ballot box instead of the coup d'etat. Nor should one doubt his sincerity in entering World War I not just to protect and enhance U.S. interests but to "make the world safe for democracy." World War II was similarly fought not just on national interest grounds but as a crusade against fascism; even today that campaign is often thought of as the last "good" war. And John F. Kennedy's Alliance for Progress should be seen as a way not just to check Soviet and Cuban expansionism in Latin America but also as a reflection of the liberal idealism of Kennedy's supporters.

In all of these instances it seems clear that hard-headed realism (expansionism, territorial aggrandizement, economic gain, bases, military victory) went hand-in-hand with moral purpose and justifications. Moral purpose and self-interest seem inseparable in the American tradition and must be wedded to achieve a successful foreign policy. Or else, moral purpose was used, concurrently or after the fact, to rationalize and justify self-interest considerations. But seldom did the moral imperative get in front of or begin to drive national interest considerations. That, in the American system, is a formula for trouble: when we begin to believe literally our own rationalizations and to conduct policy on that basis. But that is precisely what began to occur under President Jimmy Carter.

It is not the purpose here, nor is there space, to review the entire history and record of President Carter's foreign policy, particularly his human rights agenda.[6] Suffice it to say that Mr. Carter began his presidency on a high moral plane, indicating that he would not lie to the American public and that human rights would constitute the foundation of his foreign policy. Some of Carter's appointees went even farther than the president himself, elevating human rights into virtually the *only* foreign policy consideration. In the Department of State, when there were conflicts between the idealistic human rights bureau and the more realistic regional bureaus, human rights considerations, thanks to the decisions of a mediating committee headed by then undersecretary Warren Christopher, consistently sided with the human rights advocates. In a number of difficult cases—Iran, Nicaragua, Argentina, Brazil—the human rights policy seemed to run so far ahead of national interest considerations, or to ignore these altogether, that the administration was accused of "losing" these countries or else of promoting such nationalism and anti-Americanism that the human rights policy was self-defeating. That is, in the latter two cases mentioned, the policy *strengthened* military-authoritarians in power for a time by enabling them to rally nationalistic public opinion against the United States.

President Ronald Reagan's foreign policy advisers set out to change the Carter emphasis. At first they appeared to be abandoning the human rights policy altogether; soon they evolved a more sophisticated position. The strategy involved two different kinds of targets. In right-wing and authoritarian regimes such as El Salvador and others in Latin America and Asia, the policy involved pressures for democratic elections, assistance to civil society groups, and the gradual nudging of these regimes back toward the political center so as to defuse domestic discontent, make the government more stable, and deprive far-left or communist groups of their support base. In communist regimes the strategy was to use the democracy/human rights agenda (such as aid to Poland's Solidarity) to embarrass these regimes, deprive them of legitimacy, and ultimately undermine them. As added bonuses, the administration soon found that by standing for democracy and human rights it could defuse *U.S.* domestic discontent, get the Congress and the human rights lobbies to support the policy, garner allied support, and provide unity and coherence to the foreign policy bureaucracy.

President George Bush largely followed the Reagan strategy of combining democracy/human rights concerns with hard-headed realism. But he was criticized by candidate Bill Clinton in the 1992 election campaign both for mistakes in dealing with

Iraq and for giving insufficient attention to democracy/human rights issues in China and elsewhere. President Clinton vowed to reverse that course and brought with him into office many of the earlier advocates (Warren Christopher, Anthony Lake, Madeleine Albright) of Jimmy Carter's original human rights policy. He filled many assistant secretary, deputy assistant secretary, and office head positions with a new generation of policy activists more "progressive," even radical, than the generation that had designed Mr. Carter's early policy. The result during President Clinton's first two or three years was a policy emphasizing (in Albright's words) "aggressive multilateralism," sometimes at what seemed to be the cost of hard-headed U.S. national interests; "enlargement" (Tony Lake's term), which begged the question of enlargement for or toward what—presumably greater democracy and human rights; and interventions in Haiti, Somalia, and Bosnia that often seemed motivated considerably more by television coverage, unchecked idealism, domestic politics, and the desire to do "good" in the world than by considerations of the national interest. For these incursions the Clinton administration was roundly criticized, even by Democrat supporters, as following a "Mother Teresa foreign policy."[7]

Part of this renewed idealism involved a refocusing on democracy and elections in a variety of nations that had seldom, if ever, had democracy and elections before. Now of course no one can argue against democracy and elections; that is akin to arguing against God, apple pie, and motherhood. But in numerous countries—Russia, Bosnia, Haiti, Mexico, among others—the democracy/elections policy seemed to take on aspects of a moral crusade, a "missionary" effort similar to those undertaken early in the century often under U.S. Marine occupation forces to bring the benefits of U.S.-style practices and institutions to poor, presumably benighted lands. The same patronizing, condescending, even racist attitudes present early in the century were visible in this campaign. Once again the moral crusade seemed to be running ahead of realistic considerations and to be proceeding regardless of other U.S. policy considerations in these countries.

Obviously the United States prefers democracy in Russia, Bosnia, Haiti, and Mexico. That is not the issue. The issue is whether democracy is possible or likely even with U.S. efforts in these countries. And whether an ethnocentric, moralistic, heavy-handed, and excessively idealistic democracy-through-elections policy might not have the effect of destabilizing these countries rather than stabilizing them. These are countries, recall, in the cases of Russia, Haiti, and Mexico, whom America would *least* like to see destabilized because the consequences both for foreign policy (in the case of Russia) and for domestic politics (Haiti, especially Mexico) would be disastrous. For instance, even the slightest hint of instability in Mexico will send millions of Mexicans streaming toward the U.S. border rather than the "mere" tens of thousands as at present. With the best of intentions, the democracy/elections policy has the clear possibility of destabilizing Mexico—the *last* country in the world Americans should wish even inadvertently to see destabilized. Complicating the issue is the institutional apparatus of election technicians, AID and other personnel, political party assistance by the National Endowment for Democracy or NED and the Democratic and Republican parties' international affairs institutes, and networks of election observers (themselves often politically biased and/or ethnocentric) who now appear to spring *automatically* into action whenever an election is called and without the larger U.S. national interest (again, who could ever be "against" democracy?) being considered. The complications, missteps, and potentially disastrous consequences stemming from this unexamined *and virtually unexaminable* policy lie at the heart of this analysis.

The Emergence of Consensus on the Democracy/Elections Policy

The consensus on democracy and elections, as one of the three pillars of the so-called Washington consensus (the other two pillars were free trade and open markets), emerged slowly during the 1980s and 1990s. At first, President Carter's democracy/human rights policy was very controversial. As secretary of state under President Richard Nixon, Henry Kissinger had followed a more hard-headed balance-of-power policy and had frequently testified in congressional hearings against the introduction of a moral agenda into foreign policy. He argued that the United States should look solely at a country's foreign posture and not pay significant attention to its internal politics. President Gerald Ford and the Department of State had also resisted the human rights agenda when it first appeared as a serious policy issue in the mid-1970s. But a purely realistic, balance-of-power approach aligned the United States with some fairly unsavory characters: Somoza, Marcos, the Shah, Suharto, human-rights-abusing Latin American militaries. Moreover, it soon became clear that, in terms of U.S. domestic politics, foreign policy could not turn a blind eye to the plight of nuns who were raped and murdered in El Salvador, blacks in South Africa suffering under *apartheid*, or Jews and Baptists who wished to emigrate from the Soviet Union. It may be that other countries—France, for example, with its nuclear tests in the South Pacific—could conduct foreign policy completely devoid of domestic public opinion, but in the United States of America, with its long moralistic and Wilsonian tradition, that was not possible.

The democracy/human rights agenda had begun during the Vietnam War at the initiative of a handful of liberal congressmen: Senators Tom Harkin of Iowa, Edward Kennedy of Massachusetts, Alan Cranston of California, and James Abourezk of South Dakota, and Representative Donald Fraser of Minnesota. The proposal to focus U.S. foreign policy strongly on human rights also came from a coalition of anti-Vietnam War groups led by the innocuous-sounding Clergy and Laity Concerned. In 1972, in addition, Senator Henry ("Scoop") Jackson had sought to tie U.S. trade policy toward the Soviet Union to a willingness on the part of the Soviets to allow dissident Jews, Christians, and others to emigrate. The human rights agenda was generally supported by liberal Democrats and opposed by the Republican administrations then in power (Nixon and Ford) as constituting unwarranted congressional interference in the president's foreign policymaking authority and as meddling in the internal affairs of other nations. The policy remained very controversial during President Carter's administration.

But succeeding Republican administrations discovered that

the democracy/human rights agenda, which they had previously denounced as romantic idealism, could be used as an effective instrument in the Cold War. In El Salvador, the democracy initiative helped bring to power centrist democrat José Napoleon Duarte, which gave the United States a moderate, elected government with which it could effectively deal, as opposed to the earlier "evil choices" of supporting a rapacious military regime or allowing the leftist guerrillas to win. In Poland through Lech Walesa and Solidarity and in Russia as well, the administration discovered that it could use democracy and human rights as a way to delegitimize and help destabilize communist regimes. Plus the policy had the added bonuses noted earlier of defusing congressional criticism, reducing allies' criticism, and providing domestic policy coherence. In other words, Democrats often supported the policy for one set of reasons (humanitarian concerns) and Republicans for another (strategic), but they both supported the policy. This was the beginning of the domestic consensus on the democracy/human rights agenda.

By the 1990s, with the collapse of the Soviet Union and the end of the Cold War, two additional features of the emerging consensus became apparent. First, the failure and eventual collapse of such economies as the Soviet Union, Eastern Europe, Cuba, and Nicaragua revealed the bankruptcy of Marxist-Leninist ideas for managing national economies. With distinct variations, capitalism, free markets, and the idea of neoliberalism emerged triumphant in the economic sphere, just as democracy had clearly triumphed in the political sphere. In addition, armed with the arguments of professional economists that showed a multiplier effect from lowering tariff barriers, and spurred on by the realization that both Europe and Asia seemed to be moving in the direction of regional trading blocs that might at some levels exclude the United States, the United States itself began to advocate a free trade bloc encompassing North and Latin America. The older high-tariff, Third World model of ISI (Import-Substitution Industrialization) underwent severe criticism for having outlived its usefulness or for having produced deleterious consequences. In its place came a new economic model—one that had earlier been championed by Margaret Thatcher, Helmut

Kohl, Ronald Reagan, and others but that now, with the end of the Cold War and the discrediting of both Marxism-Leninism and ISI, triumphed seemingly *everywhere*–that emphasized both open markets and free trade.

Hence, by the early 1990s, and certainly by the time of the Miami Summit of December 1994 that brought together the heads of state of all the Western Hemisphere countries save Cuba, what was now being called the "Washington consensus" was firmly in command. The consensus consisted of three interrelated goals: (1) *democracy* (mainly meaning elections) and human rights; (2) *open markets*–coupled with privatization, state-downsizing; and (3) *free trade*, within a larger common-market arrangement. The interrelations of these three harked back to a long tradition of U.S. policy and foreign assistance and bore a striking resemblance to the 1960s ideas of economist, architect of the Agency for International Development, and National Security adviser W. W. Rostow.[8] That is, open markets and free trade will help improve the economy, raise living standards, create a larger middle class, and ultimately promote stability and democracy. In turn, democracy was seen as the best way to ensure stability and moderation that would guarantee a propitious climate for investment, open markets, and free trade. In addition– again in keeping with a long tradition of American thinking–all three of these pillars–democracy, open markets, free trade–were seen as complementary and as going hand-in-hand; no thought was afforded the possibility that open markets and free trade could upset stability and democracy, or that democracy might not always be the most conducive political system to a functioning, efficient economic program, particularly in developing nations' early stages of growth.

After all the disputes over U.S. foreign policy between idealists and realists during the course of the 1960s, 1970s, and 1980s, to achieve a consensus on policy in the 1990s was nothing short of remarkable. Moreover, because it is so difficult and time-consuming bureaucratically for the U.S. policymaking system to reach closure, make a decision, let alone reach consensus on *anything*, one can understand why, once reached with so much difficulty, decision-makers would be reluctant to reopen the issue.

Yet reexamination is necessary, because in many key countries the policy is not working. It is producing discord, division, and even disintegration in many societies rather than harmony, consensus, growth, and stability. In country after country–Russia, Mexico, Bosnia, Haiti–both the policy and the assumptions that undergirded it are faulty, producing unintended consequences. It is not just that the glass of policy accomplishments is both half empty and half full, which would be a comfortable belief on which to rest and go forward. Rather the policy itself is flawed because a number of its assumptions are either erroneous or mistakenly applied. In parallel studies this author and others have focused on the main economic flaws in the Washington consensus;[9] but this monograph concentrates specifically on the policy's political pillar: the democracy/elections/human rights agenda.

Overview

The following chapters examine the main areas and cases where the democracy/elections strategy has been attempted. Chapter 2 focuses on Russia, Eastern Europe, East Asia, the Middle East, and Africa. Chapter 3 examines Latin America, addressing such recent and important cases as Mexico, Haiti, Peru and Guatemala, Venezuela, and the Dominican Republic.

Chapter 4–Conclusions and Policy Recommendations–returns to the larger themes of this introduction. Building on the case study materials presented in the previous two chapters, it raises once more the issues surrounding the policy consensus on democracy, examines the diversity of democratic systems presented and also the need for a more nuanced U.S. policy, and considers the issue of reconciling democratic concerns with other U.S. interests and of coping with the many *partial* democracies in the world. It also wrestles with the problem of how to advance democracy without producing the very polarization and breakdowns of government that we seek above all else to avoid and offers some suggestions as to how to both advance democracy *and* serve U.S. interests.

It is an engaging, challenging, and provocative discussion. The goal must be both to encourage democracy and to serve U.S. policy interests at the same time. For these two—democracy and U.S. interests—are not necessarily, always, or automatically in harmony; indeed in many cases, such as the important ones examined here, they may prove incompatible, contradictory, or at cross-purposes. The goal is to bring these interests back into harmony, but the task of arriving at that end will require a far more sophisticated understanding and policy than is now available.

2

Case Studies: The Diversity of Democracy

With the triumph of the democracy agenda as part of the "Washington consensus," the United States has now put a large number of its foreign policy eggs in the democracy basket. The question raised here is: Is this a wise and prudent decision? If the bottom falls out of the democracy basket in a key country or several key countries, where does that leave U.S. foreign policy?

A series of related questions follow from and are a part of this one large, overarching question. Might not different regions and countries often mean something different by democracy than Americans do? What if their definition is *not* in accord with U.S. foreign policy goals? Or what if they practice a form of democracy that U.S. human rights lobbying groups cannot accept—or that the now institutionalized elections/democracy observer groups cannot certify as "democratic" by U.S. standards? Instead of enhancing stability, which is the assumption of the policy, suppose the elections that the United States supports prove to be divisive, produce chaos, and tear a country apart? Or suppose they bring to power a movement or party inimical to U.S. interests? Instead of enhancing regime legitimacy—another purpose of the policy—perhaps the elections the United States supports weaken legitimacy and cause a rending of the social fabric. Or perhaps, as in Bosnia, to cite a concrete example, the elections that the United States promotes as an act of reconciliation and unification instead serve to ratify the already existing partition of that country, sharpening ethnic divisions and rancor rather than promoting peaceful pluralism? These are the kinds of questions that the following case studies—dealing with Russia, China/Asia, Eastern Europe/ Bosnia, Islamic society, Africa, and Latin America (treated in chapter 3)—seek to answer.

For the fact is, the democracy initiative in U.S. foreign policy provides both an opportunity and a trap. If handled well and sensitively, with due pragmatism and taking account of the diverse meanings and understandings of democracy in countries other than our own, the democracy program can be a decided plus for U.S. policy. But if handled badly, ethnocentrically, without regard for or sensitivity to the distinct meanings of democracy in different parts of the globe, or if used—a real danger—mainly to satisfy *domestic* political constituencies and in ways that run roughshod over other countries' ways of doing things, then the democracy initiative has the potential to produce a series of disasters. I believe we are at this moment right on the edge of producing the latter rather than the former result.

Russia

From at least the times of Peter the Great and Elizabeth the Great, Russia has been torn between its Westernizing and its Slavophile tendencies. Is Russia a Western country and does it wish to be Western, or is it something else: Slavic, Eurasian, indigenous Great Russian? These disputes *between* Russians and *within* the Russian soul did not die out under communism; indeed at some levels Russian communism may be viewed as a way of both accepting (Marx was, after all, a Westerner) and repudiating the West. And clearly in present-day Russia this dispute is very much alive: whether to embrace the West and all that it stands for (including democracy and elections) or to reject Western influences and go in its own (still undetermined) nationalistic directions.[1] The issue is complicated in the Russian case because in the post-Soviet era nationalism has been associated with the revival of communism and, therefore, causes major strategic concern to the West.

At least five times in previous history Russian leaders have sought to integrate Russia into the West by bringing Western ways to Russia. Each prior effort has ended in failure, a fact that augurs ill for present efforts. Those Russian leaders who have attempted to bring in Western institutions and practices have been revered on the one hand and castigated on the other for violating Russian nationalism and for attempting to impose an inappropriate, ill-fitting Western model on a Russian society where it fails to fit or fits only uncomfortably. Moreover, these efforts are not just neutral in a policy sense—that is, a social science laboratory experience without consequences—for invariably the efforts to Westernize Russia have not produced happy stability, progress, and democracy, but chaos. This chaos and the reaction to it usually give rise to new currents of anti-Westernism, which have invariably ended in nationalistic dictatorships—precisely what the United States and its allies would now like to avoid. This debate between Westernization and indigenous nationalism, which has waxed in Russia for more than 300 years, is, according to the great Russian novelist Leo Tolstoy, the most important of all Russian controversies.[2]

Since the collapse of the Soviet Union, U.S. policy has been based on the mistaken assumptions that Russia could follow the U.S. development path, that it wanted a democratic political system and a free economy just like ours, and that all that was required was some economic pump-priming on our part and—although the road might be a bit rocky at times—Russia would soon blossom into a middle class, free market, and democratic society resembling ours. These assumptions were likely reinforced by the fact that many Western observers of Russia (journalists, academics, embassy officials) *wanted* these developments to happen or that their contacts and experiences were mainly focused in Moscow and on groups (intellectuals, fellow journalists, et cetera) that *are* Western-oriented.

But policy cannot be based on wishful thinking or on unrepresentative samples. Nor is it clear that Russia unambiguously wants democracy and free markets, or wants them all that much, or in the American form. Nor should we interpret Russia as merely a less-developed country bound to imitate the Western model, for Russia has virtually no base or foundation for doing so. Russia never experienced the Renaissance, the revolution of religious diversity and pluralism, the Enlightenment, the English revolution of limited government, the industrial revolution, or the gradual development of liberalism and freedom that were important ingredients in the rise of Western democracy and free economies. Lacking these foundations, Russia should not be expected to imitate the West, however palely; Russia represents perhaps an *alternative* route to modernization but not just a faint echo of the Western experience. Democracy and free markets in this context must be built from scratch, and the process will be very long (two to three generations) and the foundational structure weak or nonexistent.

The United States and Western Europe have tried to tie Russia to the West, to envelop Russia within a Western-style democratic system and regime. This policy of taming and civilizing the Russian Bear was intended to defuse the explosive, disintegrative forces in Russia, control and dismantle its nuclear capacity, and bring Russia in as a partner rather than a hostile enemy in international disputes. All the massive foreign aid, diplomacy, technical advising, consultations, foreign exchanges, and military cooperation have been aimed at this overriding goal. The U.S. elections/democracy initiative has constituted a major part of the goal in its wedding of moralism and self-interest. But because the U.S. policy of assisting elections by its very nature involves the United States in internal Russian affairs, and because the policy has seemed at times to favor Boris Yeltsin over democracy considerations per se, the policy itself has become controversial. Although it has aided the electoral process, it has also stimulated greater Russian resentments in some quarters over the intervention of "outside powers" and fueled the very anti-Western sentiments the policy was designed to overcome.

The particular beneficiary of the U.S. elections strategy has been Yeltsin. After he helped lead the countercoup in 1991 that definitively removed hard-line communists from the center of power and was pictured riding on the tank in defense of Russia's newly won freedoms, he gained the image of a heroic figure who was a stalwart of democracy. His 1996 presidential electoral victory over communist challenger Gennadii Zyuganov, in which Yeltsin won an unexpectedly large percentage of the vote, cemented his credentials as the best hope for democracy, freedom, and a close working relationship with the West.

But Yeltsin's are a precarious set of shoulders on which to rest U.S. policy hopes both for democracy in Russia and the cementing of ties to the West. His health is precarious. His drinking habits (not unusual in Russian culture, maybe even increasing his popularity and electability there) compounded his health problems and, during his binge drinking, all but paralyzed the Russian government for days or weeks at a time. Moreover, although these are downplayed by U.S. officials, Yeltsin himself demonstrates frequent authoritarian and not-very-democratic tendencies that make him not all that different from his main rivals and often belie the image we have of him as a democratic leader. During my research in Russia, Yeltsin was seen by informed voters as purely a transitional figure—but transitional to what was not clear. It could be either democracy *or* a restored nationalistic authoritarianism. Nowadays, these same informed voters hope only that Yeltsin's health remains stable so that he can hang on and provide continuity for another year or two—long enough in these voters' view to help stabilize the political system and allow new leaders to emerge.

The 1996 election in Russia did not produce the hoped-for democratic stability that U.S. officials wanted but may have had the opposite result. Yeltsin's health problems and ineffective leadership have caused power to drain away to often unscrupulous advisers. The challenge from the hardliners forced Yeltsin to dismiss most liberals from his government. Meanwhile, the prime minister and the secret police seem to be setting up parallel, unelected governments that often ignore or defy the president. Rather than the election cementing democracy, since 1996 Russia has moved *away from* democracy. At the same time, the policy process is paralyzed: waiting as usual for leadership from the all-powerful state, the long-suffering Russian population is becoming increasingly frustrated because few decisions are being made. Yeltsin's ill health combined with the state's financial straits and its uncertainty about how and where to lead all add to the paralysis and lack of progress.

Apart from Yeltsin—and it is telling that so many of our policy hopes for Russia rest on the shoulders of this one man whose own future seems so fragile—Russian democracy and its ties to the West remain extremely uncertain. The rule of law is still precarious, property rights are ill-defined and often abused, and a solid, stable middle class has yet to emerge. The country is woefully underdeveloped economically; east of Moscow, Russia is more akin to such other uncertain Third World giants as Brazil, Mexico, or India than it is to the developed nations of Western Europe or North America. Virtually every social sector or institution in Russia—agriculture, industry, education, health care, social programs, the family, morality, transportation, the armed forces, housing—have disintegrated badly since communism lost power and are *only beginning* to reconstitute themselves under new auspices. Crime, corruption, violence, and general brutishness have reached epidemic proportions as the social and political controls of the old regime have collapsed. And the new institutions championed by the United States and the West—political parties, nongovernmental organizations (NGOs), "civil society"—are still only weakly institutionalized and are largely limited to Moscow and the Western areas of Russia. Lacking deep roots in the Russian soil, these often artificial creations of U.S. foreign assistance may be incapable of surviving on their own and are used by unscrupulous Russians to milk the West of its money but with meager positive results.

Within Russia as well as among foreign observers there is now considerable debate as to whether Russia is over the hump. This is a judgment call, impossible to determine definitively, and therefore still open to discussion. On the one hand, the economy is doing slightly better, food is plentiful albeit expensive, and Russian society seems to be settling down. There are even arguments that Russian democracy is sufficiently strong that it can survive Yeltsin's incapacitation or death. A new constitution was adopted in December 1993 that is still, despite ups and downs, governing the rules of the political game; and elections are becoming the rule by which power changes hands. Believers in this optimistic picture ask what additional steps Russia needs to take to "prove" to the West that it is truly democratic.

But the weaknesses of Russian democracy and the political, social, and economic system more generally are also plain to see. After all, the collapse of communism was less than a decade ago. The country's newer institutions and market-oriented economy are still weak and precarious. Polls in early 1996 showed only 10 percent of Russians believe the country is headed in the right direction. Many social, economic, and political institutions, as well as the Russian military and the state itself, continue to show at least as many disintegrative features as reintegrative ones. The leadership, which remains thin, is not necessarily committed to Western democratic values. There are too many political parties, and nostalgia for the stability and certainty of the old regime abounds. The possibility exists that the communists could come back to power by electoral means.

Up to a point, the West's strategy toward Russia has been successful. A power vacuum has not so far developed in the Kremlin, the country has not completely fallen apart, Russia has been generally cooperative heretofore on the international front, and the nuclear weapons arsenal has mainly been kept under control. Moreover, one can say that the elections/democracy strategy has given greater legitimacy to Yeltsin's leadership in Moscow. So far the lid has been kept on a situation that is potentially explosive and very dangerous (given all those weapons of mass destruction). It is possible that no more could or should be expected from the policy.

And yet the unknowns and disintegrative forces are sufficiently strong that they remain worrisome. Certainly the policy offers little grounds for complacency, let alone triumph. It remains an open question whether the legitimacy conveyed on recent Russian governments and particularly on the person of Yeltsin by the elections strategy will in the long term outweigh the deep divisions the elections strategy has introduced into the Russian body politic. It is hard to tell if the economy has now "turned a corner" as the supporters of the policy believe, or if it is still degenerating into "crony capitalism," unprecedented graft, and inside favoritism. There are reports, for instance, that indicate that upwards of *90 percent* of the vast patrimony that is (or was) the huge public sector in Russia has been squandered through corruption, a figure that makes earlier (and eventually short-lived) corrupt regimes like Batista's, Marcos's, Somoza's, or the Shah's look like pikers by comparison. Nor is it certain that the newer political parties, interest associations, and NGOs ("civil society") have a genuine life of their own or if they remain purely the creatures of Western assistance programs, meant to siphon off Western assistance money but without leaving a genuinely democratic infrastructure in place.

The elections strategy, rather than unifying the country and providing legitimacy to its government, may have served to polarize the electorate into two large camps or "families": those who have profited from the recent Westernization (relatively few in numbers) and those who have not—and who are resentful besides. Many Russian liberals and democrats, having been ousted from Yeltsin's inner circle and looking at the resurgence of the communists as well as the rising authoritarianism in the government, are losing heart; even worse, they tend to blame the Russian people, who are both long-suffering but also increasingly impatient, for the failures to solidify democracy, saying that the weight of both Czarist history and Soviet totalitarianism has created an ignorant, brutish rabble for whom democracy is ill-suited.[3] Polls are clearly showing a discouragingly high *and growing* support for authoritarian values and a strong statist-populist-nationalist solution.[4] Hence, the "new Russia" seems to be a strange beast: partly Asiatic, partly Western, partly Slavic, and all Russian; partly communist and partly capitalist; proud and resentful at the same time; both dynamic and sluggish; both democratic at some levels and authoritarian at others.

At the least, these mixed tendencies should oblige us to remain skeptical of the claims for success for its Russia policy emanating from the U.S. embassy in Moscow and from the executive branch in Washington. Such claims were meant at least as much to make U.S. policy look successful through the 1996 U.S. election as to reflect the realities of the situation in Russia. At a higher level, and when combined with evidence from other countries and areas, these comments may oblige us to rethink the entire elections/democracy strategy, as well as the policy of resting so many policy hopes on the weak reed of Yeltsin's leadership.

China and Asia

In the past, the United States regarded much of Asia as an underdeveloped or developing area. But in recent decades Asia's economic successes—first in Japan; then in the "Four Tigers" of South Korea, Taiwan, Hong Kong, and Singapore; more recently in Indonesia, Thailand, Malaysia, the Philippines, and giant China—have forced a rethinking of earlier assumptions. Moreover, economic success has given Asia greater assertiveness in international affairs, including the assertion of a distinct "Asian model" of development.[5] And within that Asian model considerable skepticism has been expressed by some Asian leaders (often with quiet support from many other countries in the region) as to the appropriateness of "Western" (read, U.S.)-style democracy within the Asian context.

At some levels, the critiques of the Western model as expressed by Asian leaders can be viewed as the rationalizations of authoritarian regimes, of not-very-democratic politicians who do not want to be bothered by the "inconveniences" of the ballot box and human rights considerations. When the critiques came from the People's Republic of China, former Prime Minister Lee Kuan Yew of Singapore, or Prime Minister Mahathir Mohamad of Malaysia, fuel is added to the charge of rationalizations to cover authoritarian practices because these *are*, in varying degrees, authoritarian regimes. But at other levels one must pay serious attention to the Asians' charges of the inappropriateness of *U.S.-style* democracy in the very different Asian political, cultural, economic, and historical setting. Moreover, when the claim of Asian "distinctiveness" is also raised by persons whose democratic credentials are impeccable and by a wealthy, successful, and powerful nation like Japan, we must take them seriously indeed.[6]

The Asian model of development, which has achieved truly

"miracle" growth rates in several nations and is now spreading throughout most of the region, is, after all, both an economic and a political model. Economically the Asian model argues for a strong state role in directing and supporting a policy of economic growth, some state subsidies of key industries, close collaboration between business and government, efficient production as well as close attention to market research, and export-led growth. But there is a strong political component to the Asian model as well, which includes a bureaucratic model of the polity and strong state decision-making, an organic conception of state-labor-employer relations that stresses unity and avoids conflict, weak labor unions, and limits on popular participation in decision-making. The model also includes a democratic but constrained political process that gives limited power to parties, parliament, and electorate while investing strong power in the bureaucracy and in bureaucratic–private sector collaboration (Japan) or that is (or was) frankly authoritarian (Taiwan, South Korea, Singapore, Hong Kong, Indonesia, the Philippines, Malaysia, virtually all the rest) until recently.[7]

Many of these conceptions of the proper ordering of economic and political organization derive from a Confucian cultural and historical tradition.[8] At one point, in Max Weber's famous turn-of-the-century study of comparative religions, Confucianism was seen as a *barrier* to economic development.[9] But now Confucianism is seen in a quite different light. With its stress on self-discipline, hierarchy, order, education, societal consensus, bureaucratic decision-making, and organic unity, Confucianism is viewed as one of the key ingredients in Japanese—and, more generally, East Asian—development.

But look again at the values emphasized in the Confucian ethos and political culture: discipline, hierarchy, order, consensus, organic unity. *All* of these are not only useful in a national development strategy, they are also very conservative values. Moreover, they can easily provide a justification for authoritarianism in the political sphere and statism in the economic arena. Indeed, the Confucian political culture may be one of the most important explanations both for the East Asian development success stories *and* for the organicism, corporatism, and centralized, bureaucratic authoritarianism that is still pervasive in the area.

There have been actually two stages in East Asian development over the past four decades. The first stage was, quite frankly, authoritarian – or at least more authoritarian than democratic. The paradigm cases are South Korea under military rule, Taiwan under the Kuomintang, Singapore under Prime Minister Lee, the Philippines under Marcos, and Indonesia under Sukarno. By a bit of a stretch (left wing versus right wing), the People's Republic of China could also be considered in the authoritarian category. So, in a sense, could Japan: democratic at some levels albeit the form imposed by an occupation (U.S.) army, and Confucian-Shintoist at other levels, especially in the critical arenas of bureaucratic decision-making, the integration of public and private realms, top-down authority, and a quasi-mercantilist economy. Authoritarianism was seen as a way of maintaining order, enforcing discipline, maintaining labor peace, and preserving social and political harmony and integration during the critical early phases of development.

But once these early, potentially disruptive phases are passed, a number of East Asian regimes have felt that they could relax the controls somewhat and provide for larger degrees of democracy. This is the second, more recent phase, of Asian development. The pressures to do so have come from both the domestic and the international environment. The paradigm cases in these regards are South Korea, Taiwan, and the Philippines. Mainland China, although still officially Marxist-Leninist, is a more decentralized and open society than before; Japan is also more democratic (but still, often uncomfortably, not Western liberal-pluralist) than it was 20 years ago. Other Asian countries may or seem to be following suit. They are all now more prosperous than before, their middle classes are larger, their people more literate, and their institutions stronger. Hence, they feel they can now relax the authoritarian controls in force for so long and move toward greater pluralism and democratization in ways that would not have been possible during their formative modernization in earlier decades.

Nevertheless, limits still exist on how far and how quickly democratization will be permitted to go; these limits also help explain the recent assertion of a distinct East Asian model of development. At least six modal patterns may be observed. First, some regimes, like that of Prime Minister Lee in Singapore, have maintained authoritarian controls longer than could be justified by internal or external threats to stability. Second, some regimes, like South Korea's or Taiwan's, have undergone democratization but kept authoritarian controls "in reserve." Third, in Japan and elsewhere, democratization has been largely confined to the political (and less important?) sphere; decision-making in the more important economic sphere has been kept closed, organic, centralized, top-down, and "Confucian." A fourth pattern, related to the above, has been the transition in several countries from a more traditional and authoritarian form of *state corporatism* to a newer, more open form of societal or *neo-corporatism* – but still within a corporatist and statist institutional framework.[10] The fifth case is China: still Marxist-Leninist at least officially and politically but at the same time rushing pell-mell toward decentralization and capitalism economically.

The sixth pattern involves the actual assertion of a distinct East Asian model of development. It behooves us to listen to some of these voices seriously. Singapore's permanent secretary of foreign affairs Kishore Mahbubani, for instance, eschews Western-style individualism, confrontation, and unchecked liberalism in favor of Asian social harmony, sense of community, and consensus.[11] He also sees a strong relation between the West's excessive individualism and freedom, and its rising crime, delinquency, poor economic performance, and societal unraveling. Many Asians voice opposition to U.S. efforts, as in China, to tie trade preferences to human rights performance, arguing that better human rights will grow *naturally* out of greater economic development.[12] Singapore's ex-Prime Minister Lee has similarly ascribed Asia's recent successes to values based on Confucianism (in his view, the family, respect for authority, a belief in consensus, and a willingness to put society's interests before the individual's), which he then contrasts with the West's excessive permissiveness. Dr. Mahathir of Malaysia in a parallel vein has critiqued the

West's "imposition" of its values on Asia while not paying sufficient attention to its own societal breakdown. Nor are these
critiques of the West and the assertion of an Asian model limited
to the "unhappy" authoritarians of China, Singapore, and Malaysia; Japan's Prime Minister Morihiro Hosokawa has similarly
stated that "it is not proper to force a Western or European-style
democracy onto others."

These sentiments have spread throughout Asia. They now
resonate in *all* countries. They are not limited to a few countries
or politicians who wish to use the "Asia model" argument as a
way of avoiding democracy and human rights. Rather, these ideas
of Asia's "superiority" and the West's "decadence" reverberate
widely through the region. They are fueled, of course, by the
undoubted successes of Asian economic development and by the
corresponding tepid growth in the West, coupled with what Asia
perceives as Western social, political, and moral decay. Let us
admit there is some truth to these charges. They may not and
need not force us to abandon our belief in democracy, pluralism,
human rights, and free markets. But they should oblige us to pay
serious attention to what is good and useful in the Asian model
and, at the same time, to be somewhat modest in the assertion of
an American model claiming to fit all countries and all culture
areas at all times.

Eastern Europe

The area for a long time known as Eastern Europe is both *a part
of* "the West" and *apart* from it. In this sense, Eastern Europe has
a great deal in common with Southern Europe (Greece, Portugal,
Spain, perhaps Italy, too). Although a part of Europe historically
and geographically, both areas for a long time were apart from it
politically, economically, sociologically, culturally, even psychologically. The question is now: Can the democracy/elections
strategy (as well as promises of NATO membership, which is
only open to democratic countries) be used to integrate Eastern
Europe permanently and peacefully into the Western family of
democratic nations?

First, we must distinguish between countries and also get our nomenclature straight. Poland, the Czech Republic, Slovakia, and Hungary (the "Visegrad four") look so far to be the most successful countries in implementing democracy; Romania and Bulgaria have made important *transitions* to democracy but have not yet *consolidated* democracy; Albania has degenerated into chaos and fragmentation; and the countries of the former Yugoslavia (Slovenia, Croatia, Serbia, Bosnia) require further differentiation and are a separate case in their own right. In addition, many of the countries named above like to think of themselves now as part of "Central Europe" while the category of "Eastern Europe" has been pushed farther east to include (depending on who's counting) Lithuania, Latvia, and Estonia, and perhaps Ukraine and Belarus as well.[13] This essay, however, will hold to the more traditional definition of Eastern Europe as encompassing Poland, the Czech Republic, Slovakia, Hungary, Romania, Bulgaria, Albania, and the former Yugoslavia.

A second preliminary point to emphasize is the enormous *differences* (as well as the similarities) between the nations of Southern Europe and those of Eastern Europe. This point is important because in much of the transition-to-democracy literature, as well as in many policy discussions, the assumption is that Eastern Europe can—relatively easily—repeat the impressive democratizing experiences of Southern Europe. But this literature and policy thinking often ignore the immense differences between these two areas. By almost any index, Southern Europe had a much firmer foundation for making a successful transition to democracy than Eastern Europe. The countries of Southern Europe have a considerably higher standard of living than do those of Eastern Europe; they have stronger, more diversified economies and a much larger middle class. In addition, the nations of Southern Europe have a far stronger associational life (political parties, interest groups—"civil society"), their political and governmental institutions are stronger, and they have larger pools of well-trained democratic leaders. Southern Europe's political culture, unlike Eastern Europe's, was psychologically preparing for its transitions to democracy long before the old regimes (Salazar-Caetano, Franco, the Greek colonels) had toppled or faded away. In addition, Southern Europe was already capitalistic and nascently pluralist; it did not have Eastern Europe's problem of having to go through a combined social, economic, and political transformation quickly and all at once. By almost any criteria (economic, social, political, values, institutions) Southern Europe was better prepared for the transition to democracy—and, it is no accident, has fared better at it—than Eastern Europe.

A major worry is that some countries in Eastern Europe may have been launched on a path to democracy before they were sociologically ready for it. This is not to say that Eastern Europe is ill-suited to democracy or that democracy is "unnatural" or unattainable there. But it is to say that the democracy campaign in Eastern Europe may have been launched when the conditions were not particularly propitious, or before the socioeconomic, political-cultural, and institutional foundations had been sufficiently laid so as to *increase the odds* that democracy could not only survive but flourish. There are no hard-and-fast preconditions for democracy, and some countries that are relatively poor (Costa Rica, Chile, Uruguay) nevertheless have strong democratic institutions. Although no *causative* relationship exists between democracy and prosperity, democracy and various socioeconomic variables, or democracy and a well-established associational and institutional infrastructure, there are clearly *correlations* between these factors and democracy.[14] In Eastern Europe far more so than in Southern Europe, these correlations have been weak; it is no accident, therefore, that democracy in Eastern Europe still rests on quite weak, sometimes even precarious, grounds as well.

In the six East European countries (the former East Germany is a special case) once joined strategically under the Warsaw Pact, it is not clear that the democracy/elections agenda has served them particularly well. The promise of democracy and improved human rights and massive allied support (including the Pope's!) to Poland's Solidarity Movement were useful in prying these countries away from the Soviet Union and in opening up the *possibilities* for democracy, but in several of the countries democracy is not working very well and may be contributing to the problems. The Czech Republic is quite solidly democratic, but Slovakia's democracy is shaky and increasingly authoritarian;

Hungary has a massive foreign debt and serious ethnic divisions; and Poland has elected a genial ex-communist as prime minister. Poland is no longer a totalitarian country under the Soviet boot, and obviously under democratic rules one has to acquiesce in the government that people freely elect. Nevertheless, an area-wide reversion to communism (including conceivably in Russia), even in its "neo," "former," and elected versions, is not exactly what the United States had in mind when it began the democracy program.

Northeast Europe, although not without its problems, seems safe for a kind of democracy for now, but Southeast Europe remains much more problematic. Romania remained under the control of Ion Iliescu, the former top communist who had governed the country since 1989. His so-called Party of Social Democracy is the haven for most of the country's former communist leaders. Although Iliescu's party was defeated in 1996, the country remains disorganized and chaotic. It has moved ahead on only limited fronts since the disintegration of the Warsaw Pact. Inflation is running at 45 percent, the management of foreign exchange has been disastrous, corruption is widespread, and social programs have disintegrated.

Bulgaria is also led by ex-communists, similarly rebaptized as "social democrats." Bulgaria has taken few steps toward opening its economy to private entrepreneurship and, as in Russia, most of the privatization has gone into the hands of communists associated with the old regime. Corruption and incompetence have reached epidemic proportions; the economy is a disaster area and offers no hope of admission into a broader Europe anytime soon. In neither Romania nor Bulgaria have elections addressed any of these countries' major problems; indeed they may have worsened the national situation by giving "democratic legitimacy" to regimes that are not always very democratic.

Further south to the former Yugoslavia, Slovenia is in better shape both politically and economically than either Romania or Bulgaria and is more Western. But Croatia is creaking and not very democratic under its leader Franjo Tudjman, while Serbia seems to be facing the options after its 1996 elections of either greater authoritarianism or national disintegration. Meanwhile

Bosnia remains a major problem area—and one of the leading test cases for the thesis that elections and *forced* (from the outside) democracy may lead a country to be worse off rather than better. Bosnia is a nation torn asunder by civil war and conflict, a nation where long memories of past atrocities combine with long swords and a powerful sense of vengeance. Indeed, Bosnia is so internally fragmented, its history as a nation so short and unhappy, and its ethnic hatreds and divisions so deep that it is hard to describe Bosnia as a nation at all.

Into this divided, fractured, brutalized, and war-torn nation, after much internal as well as international debate and *angst* as to the feasibility of outside intervention, came the United States and its NATO allies. They agreed to send in peace-keeping forces and, as part of the Dayton Peace Accords, to supervise democratic elections. The peace-keeping has gone well but the civic, nation-building, and elections strategies have not. The elections were intended to help reunify the country and provide the elected government with a degree of democratic legitimacy. But instead they (1) strengthened the geographic divides already present; (2) reinforced the ethnic divisions already polarizing the country; (3) fell victim to widespread electoral manipulation and fraud; (4) revealed again the deep-seated degrees of hatred, bitterness, and lack of communication among all groups; and (5) failed to provide the legitimacy that the elected government and the outside sponsors of the elections had hoped for.

The result of the election in Bosnia is the de facto partition of the country. The powerful Serb and Croat elements in the population have had their power and that of their leaders confirmed, while the weaker Muslims have again been left on the outside looking in. A democratic figleaf, useful for U.S. domestic political purposes, has been provided to this partition, but no more than a figleaf. Meanwhile, the contradiction that was at the heart of the U.S. policy at the beginning continues unresolved: either step aside and allow the current de facto partition to proceed, or intervene massively as a way of setting the country in a new democratic direction. But neither the U.S. administration nor the NATO allies have been willing to pay the political costs of either of these other options, preferring instead a partial and limited role that involves limited risks and limited costs. But that "safe" role has not solved the Bosnia problem and may have exacerbated it.[15]

The elections held in Bosnia in September 1996 were peaceful enough and, at least on election day, technically satisfied the criteria of "fair and honest"; but the mere casting of ballots does not mean the ethnic rivals can live side by side. The elections were projected to create a functioning and pluralist country from three, deeply hostile ethnic factions; but in fact each group sought to manipulate the election, not to encourage peaceful pluralism but to consolidate its own position for a future showdown with a hated neighbor. Massive pressures and intimidation were used by each group to try to achieve an outcome favorable to themselves; each group suppressed dissent within its own area, controlled the press, and prevented the free movement of peoples that the Dayton accords called for. The result was not an expression of popular will that could shore up and legitimize a functioning Bosnian government but mainly tactical positioning by the ethnic parties for the continuing conflict that all saw ahead.

Although the national elections were held on schedule – chiefly to satisfy the political requirements of the occupying forces – municipal elections had to be postponed. Municipal elections in Bosnia are even more fractious and fraught with danger than national elections. They involve even more questions about freedom of movement and residency, and all the parties, again, want to use the elections to ratify the gains they had earlier made politically and on the battlefield. Moreover, West European diplomats were even more emphatic than they had been on the national election that local elections would create more problems than they would solve. The United States reluctantly agreed, lauding the national election as demonstrating the "success" of the policy but bowing to pragmatic realities on the issue of the municipal elections – even though the corruption and manipulation present at the municipal election level were also present at the national level.

The unpleasant facts must be faced: the Dayton plan for elections in Bosnia was little more than a public relations gambit to atone for earlier policy failures and to make the West "look good" by "standing for" democracy and elections. Who can oppose those goals, however hollow and unrealistic they may be in the Bosnian context? But looked at more closely the policy has the elements of a sham: massive abuses in voter registration rolls, none of the promised freedom of movement for potential voters, limited freedom of expression, and indicted criminals manipulating the process from behind the scenes, with the West's acquiescence, to maintain themselves in power, to secure their ethnic group's position for the battle that will be resumed after the election, and perhaps even to destroy the artificial creation called "Bosnia" itself by rejoining their territories to Serbia and Croatia. However, by claiming it is upholding the democratic principles laid down in Dayton, the U.S. administration could claim a foreign policy "victory" just in time for the November 1996 election. This shaky policy verges on being called fraudulent.

Islamic Society

Of the 39 Islamic countries in the world, only 6 or 7 could even remotely be called democratic, and of these, most would be described as limited or troubled democracies. The ranks of democracies among the Islamic countries include Pakistan, where democratically elected Prime Minister Benazir Bhutto has been ousted from power; Turkey, which is riven by political and ethnic differences; Jordan, a monarchy but with an elected parliament; Maylasia, which practices both democracy and authoritarianism; Bangladesh, whose sheer poverty makes democracy always precarious; and perhaps Iran—not exactly my idea of democracy—which now has an elected parliament. Among the others, Senegal, Niger, and Mali have held recent elections, but they and the rest of the Moslem states remain closer to authoritarianism than to democracy. Overall, both historically and contemporaneously, democracy has not fared well in the Islamic world.[16]

Part of the reason for the deficit of democracy among the Islamic countries is cultural and religious. The Koran, as well as Islamic law, emphasizes authority, discipline, and unquestioned obedience far more than democratic participation. It stresses the

Islamic community over individual responsibility and provides justification for an organic and theocratic state, not one emphasizing rights, pluralism, and separation of powers. The punishments that it calls for seem excessively harsh by contemporary standards; at least in its recent fundamentalist versions, it does not seem to be loving, forgiving, or redemptive.[17]

But it is not just culture and religion alone that have hindered democracy in the Islamic world. The Islamic states that emerged from colonialism after 1918 and then again after 1945 have been more oriented toward authoritarian nation-building than political freedom. Economic underdevelopment in much of the Islamic world has been another barrier to democracy. In addition, the leaders of the Islamic nations in recent times have often been strongmen, military authoritarians, and strong nationalists who have used nationalism or pan-Arabism to compensate for political and economic failings. Some of these also took to using Marxist demagoguery to justify their nondemocratic inclinations; others used the language of Islam to disguise corruption and looting. There is no single reason for the general absence of democracy among Islamic nations, nor can one say at this time that trends are inexorably pointing this part of the world in a democratic direction.

One *can* find in the Koran and in Islamic law passages and concepts that could conceivably, in the right circumstances or under the right leadership, be used to justify democracy—for example, the concept of *ijma*, or "consensus." If the Islamic community agrees on the right thing to do, then that is what should be done, and, according to Islam, a community of God cannot make an error. *Ijma* seems to contain democratic elements of community public opinion and the building of consensus. But so far it has been mainly Islamic holy men who can define this "consensus," and the rest of the community has seldom been willing to deny such power to the *mullahs*.

Another Islamic concept that could conceivably serve as a base for democracy is *shura* or "consultation." An Islamic government is supposed to consult the people about the policies it intends to follow. But what does such consultation consist of and what institutional form will it take? Not, so far in most countries, by means of regular, democratic elections. In Saudi Arabia, for example, before his health began to fail, the king would periodically take his royal tent out into the desert, consult with tribal chiefs, and often grant their petitions on demand. But this procedure depends on the health, orientation, and often whim of the monarch; it did not include regular or democratic elections; and it is closer to a patronage system of mutual "gifts" (benefits bestowed in return for loyalty) than it is to democracy. The system is closer to patrimonialism or even a military command system than it is to popular participation: he asks his subcommanders what they think but then takes all decisions unilaterally. It is hard to find a solid, consistent, and institutionalized basis for democracy in either *ijma* or *shura*.

The United States and its Western allies have not been as quick or as vocal in condemning human rights and democracy abuses in countries like Saudi Arabia, Kuwait, or the Persian Gulf emirates as in other regions. Part of that simply reflects a realistic assessment that democracy and elections have few possibilities of success here, but part of it reflects a conscious decision that Saudi Arabia and Kuwait are simply too important for other reasons— oil!—to merit overconcern about democracy/human rights considerations. The situation is comparable to U.S. attitudes toward China before the end of the Cold War: everyone knew there were widespread human rights abuses in China, but as long as the United States could play the "China card" as a way of putting added pressure on the Soviet Union, no one would talk very much about the violations there. Now, with the Cold War over and less need to play the China card, the United States does pay stronger attention to human rights in China; but unfortunately for the democracy/elections agenda, the U.S. need for Middle Eastern oil has not decreased in the same way as did the need to use China to check the Soviets. Other than an occasional embassy *démarche*, as in Kuwait after the Gulf War when international publicity focused on the country, other priorities simply take precedence over any talk about democracy and human rights in U.S. dealings with the oil-rich sheikdoms of the Gulf.

Realistically, a policy need not be 100 percent consistent in order to be a good policy. In general, the democracy/elections agenda has been a good one, worthy of continued support. But as the Saudi, Kuwait, and possibly some other cases illustrate, sometimes other important considerations and U.S. interests have to take priority over or be weighed *along with* the democracy/human rights issues.

But on the opposite side of this coin are the countries that had democratic elections but where the United States, because it did not like the outcome, declined to acknowledge or uphold their legitimacy. The primary case is Algeria. Algeria is governed by a military-authoritarian regime that, to lessen its unpopularity, allowed elections to occur in late 1991. But when the government saw which way the votes were tending—toward a victory of extremist Moslem fundamentalists—it abruptly canceled the second electoral round scheduled for early 1992. The former colonial power in Algeria, France, backed the Algerian government; the United States along with most other NATO nations backed the French decision and quietly forgot about this blatantly nondemocratic electoral violation. The logic was similar but the reverse of that governing the Saudi case: "other considerations"—in this instance the threat of a radical fundamentalist takeover—were deemed more important than preserving electoral integrity. Again one could say that a policy need not be always consistent in order to be a good policy, but how many such exceptions should be allowed before the policy itself requires examination? And in this case the policy clearly did not work: Algeria's fundamentalist rebellion has expanded and is even more violent now than before the electoral door was slammed. The country has polarized between extremes, and no middle ground appears in sight. Is it conceivable that even more important Egypt might polarize, fragment, and break down in the same manner?

Clearly for 80 percent of the 39 Islamic countries, democracy and regular elections are a long way off—and may never develop in our lifetimes or even the lifetime of the elections policy. Nearly 20 percent of all the nations in the world have thus been written off for the democratic cause—and that is in just one region or culture area alone. It is not an auspicious conclusion for a policy that claims to have universal validity.

Meanwhile, compounding the policy's difficulties, scholars

and political leaders in the Islamic countries, as in East Asia, have begun to propound a uniquely Islamic model of national development.[18] Along with that development is coming the assertion of an entire Islamic culture, history, and social science. These models will be put in contrast with the predominant Western ones: they will be wrapped in nationalism and Islamic culture and religious as well as more neutral social science formulations. The source of these models will be the Koran, Islamic law (the *Shari'a*), and recent national experiences. The stress will be on community and organicism rather than Western individualism, on a strong central state as distinct from checks and balances, on "consensus" (*ijma*) rather than contested elections, on "consultation" (*shura*) instead of genuine pluralism and democracy, on a corporately organized society as distinct from a liberal one of free associations, and on strong political authority and leadership instead of the regular turnover of officials that democracy implies.

This assertion of a native or home-grown (in this case, Islamic) ideology, system of laws, and model of development will serve not only to further frustrate the U.S. democracy/elections strategy but to offer even stronger justification and rationalization for the Islamic world to go its own way and to reject Western precepts. It may well bring to power *more* fundamentalist Islamic regimes (and certainly nondemocratic ones, by our lights) rather than less.[19] The scary feature may be that such assertions of indigenous, non-Western, nondemocratic ways of doing things are growing not just in the Islamic world but in other areas as well.

Africa

Poor Africa! Poor, crumbling, long-suffering Africa! That is the attitude of most Americans, including policymakers, toward sub-Saharan Africa—an attitude both of despair and of resignation. Americans feel sorry for Africa and wish they could help, but the problems are so deep and manifold as seemingly to defy all possibilities of solution. It is sad but there is not a lot that can be done; polls show Americans have reached a state of what is termed "donor exhaustion." These attitudes also hold on the democracy front where Africa's prospects for democratic transitions and consolidation have all but been written off. Africa seems hopeless.

Africa was not always viewed in such pessimistic terms. Immediately after that great wave of decolonization in the late 1950s and early 1960s, when a host of new African nations burst upon the world scene, the prospects seemed reasonably solid. A great deal of euphoria had accompanied independence, new and democratic constitutions had been written, and civilian leaders like Kwame Nkrumah, Sékou Touré, and Julius Nyerere seemed poised to lead Africa into a new and hopeful era. Several of these movements represented single-party systems, but in the prevailing literature of the time these were presented as integrating parties, with internal if not external democratic features, and signifying a uniquely African form of democracy.[20]

But by the mid-to-late 1960s democracy in Africa was in headlong retreat. The civilian leadership often proved corrupt or inept or both, numerous constitutions were abrogated, and a wave of military regimes replaced the early independence leaders. The political parties touted earlier as an African version of democracy proved to be purely paper organizations, lacking mass appeal or mass membership; they simply disintegrated and disappeared without a whimper under the onslaught of military authoritarianism. Then came pictures of military brutality, violence and sometimes civil war, national breakdowns, famine and starving children, widespread corruption, seeming ungovernability, and AIDS. Africa seemed like a "disaster area," a "basket case," with all the countries of the region lumped together indiscriminately under those damning epithets. American students and professors who had once planned to concentrate their careers on the area began to lose interest and drift into other subjects, membership in the African Studies Association declined precipitously, and a variety of Africa-centered journals that once provided deeper context than the everyday headlines were forced to close.

At the policy level, too, Africa received less attention and then only when one or another country served temporarily as a Cold War battleground. U.S. missions were closed or reduced in size, foreign service officers came to view an assignment in Africa as damaging to their careers and thus to be avoided, and those few State Department officials willing to take on an Africa assignment were often obliged to be apologetic about it. Eventually the policy focus shifted as well, away from democratization as a hopeful basis for policy *toward* disaster relief, humanitarian missions, and rescue efforts—all signs that countries and societies may be on their last legs. Agencies with a democracy focus like the National Endowment for Democracy, the Republican Institute for International Affairs, the Democratic International Affairs Institute, and the Agency for International Development's Democracy Office concentrated on Latin America and eventually Russia, Eastern Europe, and Asia, but paid little sustained attention to Africa. There, the prospects for democracy seemed so dismal that, without saying so explicitly, democracy groups and advocates had all but given up.

In this climate of despair and hopelessness, South Africa for a time offered a measure of promise and renewal. The opening of the political system, the abolition of *apartheid*, and the election of black leader Nelson Mandela to the presidency seemed to offer a new dawn not only in South Africa but perhaps throughout the rest of the continent as well. But by now, the euphoria has worn off the South African transition as well, and increasingly pessimistic notes are being sounded about the future of even that resource-rich country.

In the meantime, after a 30-year interval since the previous effort at democratization, and notwithstanding the depressing images of Africa on our television screens night after night, African democracy received a new impetus in the early 1990s. Elections were held in Namibia (1989), Cameroon (1992), Nigeria (1993), Kenya (1992), Congo (1992, 1993), Togo (1993), Central African Republic (1993), Gabon (1993), Senegal (1993), Cote d'Ivoire (1990), Niger (1993), Madagascar (1992, 1993), Malawi (1994), Ethiopia (1992), and Ghana (1992); more recently there have been elections in Mozambique, Zaire, Tanzania, Uganda, and Angola. The sheer number of elections suggests that Africa is not entirely without experience in elections or democracy.[21]

This *wave* of elections in the early 1990s meant that it would be another four or five years before a new round of elections would be held. But these intervening years have not been particularly kind to the cause of democracy in Africa. Much like the optimistic mood that accompanied independence in the early 1960s, the democracy movement that seemed to be progressing across Africa in the early 1990s has bogged down, for several reasons. First, quite a number of the region's autocrats and authoritarian regimes have proved to be more adept and long-lasting than expected. Second, and the reverse side of that coin, democracy movements in Africa have proven to be weaker, with a less secure social and political base, than was expected.

Moreover, the elections that have occurred have often been manipulated in undemocratic ways. In some countries (Benin, Central African Republic, Congo), democracy has meant the perpetuation of the same groups or leaders in power but under a different label. In other countries (Senegal, Ghana, Botswana, Zimbabwe), it has meant allowing minor parties to operate as "safety valves" for pent-up frustrations even while a dominant ruling party remains in power. In still a third group of countries (Togo, Zaire, Gabon, Cameroon, and perhaps Kenya as well), the holding of elections provided not a clear choice but only a means by which an incumbent autocrat could hang onto power with the added advantage of "democratic legitimacy." For a fourth group of countries (Angola, Ethiopia, Mozambique), the holding of elections provided the vehicle whereby civil war and conflict could be carried on temporarily by other means. As a result, only in a handful of cases (Malawi, Mali, Niger, Namibia, Zambia; several of these also counted under the Islamic category) has a more-or-less democratic election been followed by the effective introduction of new participants into the political process.[22]

Five or six (including South Africa) democratic "successes" in fifty-four countries (about 10 percent) is not an outstanding record. The proportion of democracies in Africa is roughly comparable to the proportion of democratic successes among Islamic countries. Neither in sub-Saharan Africa nor in the Islamic world has the recent democratic scoresheet been at all impressive.

But the problem goes deeper than that. Elections in Africa are not only often fraudulent, rigged, or meaningless; they often do downright harm to the countries experiencing them and to U.S. policy interests. In Ethiopia, for example, elections have so far been followed not by legitimate democratic governments but only by renewed internal conflict. Kenya's elections, which were praised by international observers, resulted in a parliament that was upsetting to President Daniel arap Moi, who then prorogued the legislature. In Angola elections led not to the peaceful settlement of the longtime political conflicts in that country but to a renewal of civil war. Ghana had elections that returned a sitting government to power, but it is doubtful that the electoral process gave the government any more sorely needed legitimacy than it had before. These examples suggest that it is risky to pressure African countries across the board to hold multiparty elections quickly and before conditions for elections and democracy are propitious. For if the elections are held prematurely and then fail—often the case—the result is usually a slowing or a halt and extreme damage to the democratization process. As Marina Ottaway concludes her study of elections and democracy in Africa, "elections can be a serious setback for democratization, and the presence of monitors can make things worse."[23]

At the same time, authoritarian leaders in Africa have learned to manipulate the U.S. emphasis on elections for their own political purposes. African leaders have learned that the foreign assistance agencies can be appeased and gotten off their backs by holding elections that are competitive enough to satisfy the aid donors without requiring the leaders to sacrifice any real power. For example, they may allow the opposition to meet and issue some propaganda, but one should not necessarily equate opposition to an existing regime with real democracy. Or, the election is manipulated to allow the opposition some voice and even a few seats in the government but no real power. Some African leaders have learned to speak the language of democracy either to avoid sanctions or to qualify for loans and international aid but without making more than token bows in the direction of Western-style democracy.

Some African leaders continue to be outspoken in their rejection of Western democracy as inappropriate in their context. Echoing the position that one *used* to hear in Latin America and East Asia, and in Africa in the early years of independence, they argue that competitive, multiparty elections are too divisive and disruptive for the fragile, underinstitutionalized African countries. Elections tend to tear the country apart, to reignite submerged ethnic conflict, to produce strife and even civil war. They may produce chaos, ungovernability, and breakdown—precisely the features that the U.S. elections strategy are designed to prevent. These leaders argue that none of the conditions is present that would enable democracy to take root and prosper: the middle class is too small, literacy is low, the economies are not expanding, civil society is weak. Some of these leaders (Uganda's Yoweri Museveni) argue that Western-style democracy is inappropriate for Africa, while others (Ghana's Jerry Rawlings) suggest that in times of crisis democracy may have to be curtailed or postponed. The argument in Africa is still strong that order and authority are preferable to the chaos and breakdown that often accompany democracy.[24]

Some African leaders, both academic and political, have gone beyond the above compromises to suggest an indigenous model of African development and democracy. Rejecting *all* Western influences as imported and inappropriate in their culture and circumstances, they have sought to fashion a local, home-grown set of institutions. Although there are many uncertainties in these plans, they most often involve a focus on ethnic or tribal realities rather than the imported institutions left over from colonial rule. The goal of an indigenous model of African development capable of improving governability and solving Africa's problems is undoubtedly an attractive one, but many problems remain in this conception. Not least are the questions of which indigenous institutions should be emphasized, who should decide, and what precise form they will take. Is it even possible to emphasize indigenous solutions in today's climate and reality of internationalization (Coke, rock music, and—not least—democracy); do the people really want indigenization or is this merely a romantic and unrealistic dream of the intellectual elites? Indigenization sounds attractive, but numerous problems must be resolved before it can become a practical reality.[25]

In the meantime, among those who have not given up entirely on Africa, emphases and priorities are shifting. Everyone agrees that democracy at least in its Western forms is not working. Tyrants both military and civilian have learned how to manipulate the process of "elections" even while keeping the opposition out of power. Voter rolls, the media, the economy, even national boundaries are manipulated to keep incumbents in power. Election observers who arrive to witness the actual polling often see only the final stage in the process, pronounce it "fair and honest," and thus sometimes compound the problem.

But beneath the surface of African politics, and focusing on changes besides elections, some deeper and possibly hopeful transformations are occurring. The size of the African state is often decreasing, as are the opportunities for corruption. Privatization is going forward. New elements of civil society and social movements are growing up independently of central state authority. Private entrepreneurs are playing a role. Local, indigenous, often ethnically based organizations are carrying out educational, justice, and social-service functions independent of the often corrupted central ministries. Change is going forward at grassroots levels regardless of the stagnation at the central government level.

In the face of these changes, some purists and democracy ideologues in the U.S. government and the aid agencies continue to insist on a form of democracy for Africa so pristine that it could not be found in the sponsoring countries themselves—and certainly not in Chicago, Baltimore, or Washington, D.C. Other U.S. officials have begun to take a more pragmatic stand. They have sought to redefine democracy, basing it not so much on elections and majority rule as on "power sharing." The government shares power with its main opposition for the sake of maintaining peace and avoiding the slide into breakdown that could involve an even worse scenario in the U.S. view—the need for U.S. troops in a humanitarian intervention. Angola and Mozambique provide two recent examples of the stress on power sharing or an election *combined with* power sharing, rather than on elections by themselves. But although power sharing may be a useful pragmatic response and an alternative to chaos and civil war, it also tends to deny the results of electoral outcomes where elections are also held; it may produce merely the sharing of spoils and of patronage favors among the groups that are parties to such pacts. This same tension between democratic idealism and the pragmatism that leads to the acceptance of regimes that are less than fully democratic is also present in Latin America.

3

Case Studies: Latin America

Latin America has long been the primary laboratory for U.S. social, political, and foreign policy experimentation abroad, and the current U.S. democracy/elections campaign is no exception. During the Spanish-American War of 1898, the United States became the dominant strategic power in the Caribbean region. That was followed by "dollar diplomacy," repeated Marine interventions in the countries to the south, and Woodrow Wilson's efforts to "teach" Mexico and the Caribbean how to elect "good men." Franklin D. Roosevelt's "Good Neighbor Policy," John F. Kennedy's Alliance for Progress, and Jimmy Carter's human rights policy all had Latin America as their main locus. Virtually all of the programs (agrarian reform, community development, family planning, basic human needs, now sustainable development) by which the United States has sought to stimulate social, economic, and political development in the Third World were first, or most strongly, tried out in Latin America. The democracy/elections policy is the most recent of these.

The successes of this agenda are readily apparent. Twenty years ago, fourteen of the Latin American countries were under military-authoritarian rule, and in three others the military was so close to the surface of power as to make the line between civilian and military all but invisible (thus leaving Costa Rica,

Colombia, and Venezuela as the only surviving democracies—and even they were labeled by experts as "elite-directed democracies").[1] By now these figures have been dramatically reversed; nineteen of the twenty Latin American republics are now more or less democratic, with Cuba the only exception. Moreover, along with democracy has come in Latin America a significant trend toward open markets and free trade. This is the famed triumvirate of the celebrated "Washington consensus" that we have heard so much about—democracy, open markets, and free trade. Surely the triumph of this agenda *is* cause for celebration, both in terms of American values and American interests.[2]

But all is not well at present with the Washington consensus; there are severe and widening cracks in the agreement.[3] Free trade and the expansion of NAFTA or a NAFTA-like agreement have not worked out as expected, given problems on both the U.S. and Latin American sides. Nor have open markets produced the desired results; the Mexican peso crisis, widely (but mistakenly) seen in Latin America as the result of an open-market strategy, seems to suggest to many Latin American leaders that a free market or neoliberal policy produces mainly unemployment, hardship, food riots, and national disintegration, and therefore is unviable politically. The democracy agenda—our main focus here—has not worked out quite as nicely as hoped.

It is not that the democracy emphasis is unviable or that the United States should not be for it, but the term "democracy" covers a vast range of meanings, some of which are not very attractive or in accord with U.S. interests. It shades over too many variations and distinctions, covering up a number of unattractive features. When the above figures are used for celebratory or propaganda purposes ("nineteen of the twenty countries are democratic"), it disguises and oversimplifies a great variety of trends—some good, some bad—occurring under that rubric. Hence, it is the "more or less" in that same paragraph above that concerns us here. When we say all but one of the Latin American countries are "more or less democratic," let us be happy about the democratic part of that phrase. But it is the "more-or-less" that interests us here in a policy sense.

Mexico

Mexico may be among the most important countries in the world to the United States. Mexico may be on a level with Japan, Germany, China, and Russia in terms of its importance to the United States. Certainly it is among the highest U.S. foreign policy priorities. It is not important for any real or potential security threat to the United States (Russia, China), nor is it an economic dynamo (Japan, Germany). But in terms of its ability to affect the United States, both positively and negatively, Mexico is as important as the other nations mentioned.[4]

Briefly, what are the main reasons for Mexico's importance to the United States? First, Mexico shares a 2,000-mile border, now in the process of being erased, with the United States; second, the United States and Mexico have recently entered into a partnership (NAFTA) that further erodes border impediments and, in effect, makes the United States the guarantor of Mexico's political and economic viability; third, the U.S.-Mexico border is the only place in the world where a modern, industrial, First World nation (the United States) rubs shoulders so closely with a Third World nation (Mexico) with all the problems, tensions, conflicts, and complexes that accompany such a relationship. Fourth, Mexico has not forgotten that the United States, in its nineteenth-century Western expansion called "Manifest Destiny," deprived Mexico of 40 percent of its national territory and thus, in Mexican eyes, enabled the United States to become a great and prosperous power rather than Mexico, and the bitterness and anti-Americanism still rankle in Mexico and importantly shape Mexico's foreign policy to this day.

But the main reason, encompassing many of the above factors, for Mexico's importance to the United States is growing interdependence between the two countries on a *host* of issues: oil, natural gas, trade, tourism, immigration, drugs, investment, water and irrigation, pollution and the environment, manufacturing, health care, poverty, education, social welfare, law enforcement and the justice system, etc. On all of these vast fronts, the United States and Mexico have become interdependent with each other in incredibly complex ways. There used to be an aphorism in Mexico reflecting this interdependence that when the United States sneezes, Mexico catches a cold. Now we have to amend that aphorism to say that if the United States sneezes and Mexico catches a cold (either politically or economically), then the United States in turn catches pneumonia.

Moreover, because of this complex interdependence, the United States is learning that Mexico's problems—through immigration and other influences—have a way of turning into *U.S. problems*. That is, to the extent that Mexico as a Third World nation has problems of unemployment, malnutrition, poverty, illiteracy, health care, excess population, crime, violence, drugs, etc., these have a way of becoming, through immigration as well as sheer proximity, our problems. And, through dispersal of the Mexican immigrant population, they are no longer limited to California and the American Southwest. It *obviously* is in U.S. interests to help Mexico solve all these problems *internally in Mexico* before, through immigration, they become virtually unsolvable problems (witness California's anti-illegal immigrant proposition 187) in the United States.

Recall also that Mexico is a big nation (the size of the United States east of the Mississippi) of nearly 100 million people. This compares (to select some neighboring countries that have recently figured prominently in U.S. foreign policy) to Nicaragua with 3 to 4 million persons, El Salvador with 5 million, and Haiti with 7 million. So if we think that these other countries with relatively small populations were controversial in U.S. foreign policy and their people's immigrations to the United States at the first sign of trouble caused shockwaves in the United States, imagine what a destabilized Mexico either economically or politically, with 100 million people and many of them streaming toward that unenforced and unenforceable U.S. border, would do to U.S. policy. The prospect has such immense consequences in terms both of foreign policy and domestic politics that, until recently, we have not even been willing to think about it. But think about it we must, for in the next few years Mexico could well destabilize. Because of massive corruption, immense social problems, a faltering economy, and an authoritarian political system, Mexico could well fragment rather than make a peaceful transition to democracy and free markets. I would put the odds that we can avoid that prospect at no better than 50 percent.

For a long time the United States has taken the stability of its two large neighbors, Canada and Mexico, for granted. But now Canada is deeply divided over the Quebec issue and could at some future point break up as a nation. That possibility carries immense implications for U.S. foreign policy. But Mexico could well be an even more complicated and dangerous case, involving either political or economic or social breakdown and disintegration, or all of these at once—with truly grave consequences for the United States.

Mexico had a major social revolution from 1910 to 1920 (the first of the twentieth century's great social revolutions, anticipating the Russian revolution by seven years) that largely destroyed the feudal, traditional order (military, church, oligarchy). Out of the chaos and disorder of the revolution, Mexico began in the 1920s to build a new political system based on a one-party (the Revolutionary Institutional Party or PRI) dominant regime, itself based heavily on patronage, violence, and corruption as well as a steadily expanding economic pie. This party has dominated Mexican politics for 70 years and, until the 1980s, was able to monopolize virtually all areas of national political life. Though authoritarian, it provided for a stable, orderly political system that caused few major problems for U.S. foreign policy.

In the economic sphere, too, Mexico appeared stable and increasingly prosperous. Since the 1940s Mexico had been one of the great success stories in the Third World. Its economy had been growing steadily at 4, 5, 6, even 7 percent a year. Mexico was not quite at the miracle growth rate level of Japan, Taiwan, or South Korea, but it was right up there with the world's leaders. It had taken its place as one of the most prosperous countries in Latin America, increasingly industrialized, and was on everyone's list as among the leading emerging markets (now rechristened as BEMs—Big Emerging Markets).

But then came the crash, both economically and politically. It may be recalled that it was *Mexico's* announcement in 1982 that it was bankrupt, could not pay its debts, and required a bailout that triggered the great Third World debt crisis of the 1980s—a debt crisis that still plagues many Third World countries today, including Mexico. Meanwhile, cracks were also appearing in Mexico's authoritarian but long-stable political system, as new social forces began to emerge, as the PRI's monopoly began to be breached, and as the Mexican population began to demand both greater freedom and greater choice. It is widely thought that the official party may have actually lost the 1988 election that brought Carlos Salinas de Gortari to power and managed to hang onto power only through widespread bribery, general chicanery, and vote stealing. Then in the 1990s came further political disintegration, the emergence of serious political challengers on both the left and the right, a number of high-level assassinations, guerrilla uprisings, rising drugs, corruption, and violence, and the further eclipsing of the official party apparatus (like a gigantic national patronage machine) as Mexico itself became a more complex and diversified nation.

The peso crisis of 1994 was both an economic and a political shock, and it compounded Mexico's problems. The crisis threw the Mexican economy into a tailspin, increased unemployment, devastated the middle and working classes, and so hurt the Mexican economy that it was pushed backward a full decade. The economic crisis exacerbated the political crisis by not only undermining the government in office but also delegitimizing the entire monopolistic, authoritarian, single-party political regime in power for so long. The issue is complicated by persistent stories that the U.S. embassy, fearing the destabilizing effects of a possible opposition victory in 1994, may have supported and perhaps encouraged the Salinas government's decision not to devalue the peso in the months before the election so that the official candidate of the PRI could once again win, a postponement that helped bring on an even greater crisis later in 1994 that may well have inadvertently undermined Mexico both economically and politically. Mexico is currently so precarious that my CSIS colleague Zbigniew Brzezinski has been giving speeches calling Mexico "the next Iran," by which he means unstable, polarized, potentially revolutionary, and anti-American. One hopes the provocative (and exaggerated) Brzezinski phrase does not take on the character of a self-fulfilling prophecy.

Mexico's economic *cum* political crisis flashed onto our consciousness just when the United States was gearing up its democracy/elections agenda. As a next-door neighbor, Mexico cannot help but be strongly affected by the numerous U.S. democracy initiatives and institutions, and most believe that *in the long run* Mexico will also benefit from free trade, open markets, and a democratic political system. But in the meantime there is the short term to get through, during which the United States—with the best of intentions—could well, through pressure and its immense influence, destabilize Mexico. Mexico is the last country in the world, for all the reasons given earlier, that the United States should want—however inadvertently—to destabilize.

There is no magic formula to save Mexico, but some of the problems to watch for and address include the following:

1. Many of the groups, institutions, and officials in NED, the Democratic Institute, etc., that the United States sends to Mexico as part of the democracy campaign are too young and too ideological; they often lack knowledge or experience of Mexican history and realities. There are some things that the United States can usefully do to encourage democracy in Mexico but others on which we as Americans should defer to Mexico, refusing to touch them with a ten-foot pole.

2. Many of these same groups and persons are afflicted with tunnel vision; their one-track minds are so committed to the democracy vision that they lose sight of the larger context and the multiple layers of interdependence in U.S.-Mexican relations.

3. The U.S. government may be trying to move too fast in Mexico (as in Russia). Mexico has been an authoritarian, top-down, corporatist, and patronage-dominated country for 500 years, and it will not change overnight. Americans often expect change to occur here and elsewhere in three to four years; three to four generations is more likely.

4. Americans often forget that Mexico has been a one-party dominant regime for 70 years; its system of *institutionalized au-*

thoritarianism is (like Russia's) deeply entrenched in the political system, reaching from national leaders to local political bosses. Because it is not just the one-man authoritarianism present elsewhere in Latin America, Mexico's beaueaucratic authoritarianism will require much more time and much greater pain if a transition to democracy is to occur.

5. Mexico's older corporatist and authoritarian institutions, which are already declining and unraveling, are gradually being replaced by interest groups of free associability and by democratic institutions. But this has to be a gradual transformation. I do not think it is appropriate for the United States to hasten that process; indeed, U.S. actions, unless prudent, could well result in the worst of all possible worlds: old institutions in Mexico destroyed and undermined before newer, democratic ones have become consolidated, leaving Mexico with a vacuum of institutions producing anarchy and ungovernability.

6. Mexico requires slow evolution, not precipitous change. Democracy is undoubtedly good for Mexico in the long run but it could, if pushed too strongly or precipitously, produce chaos in the short term that would prove disastrous to U.S. interests. Moreover, Mexican democratization must be led and defined by Mexico, not by the United States. Mexico is the case *par excellence* that too rapid democratization, too sharp a break with the past, pushed by well-meaning but naive Americans, could be disastrous both for Mexico and the United States.

To be honest and realistic, Mexico is in bad trouble both politically and economically. The problems may be getting worse rather than better. Now, if the United States makes a mistake and by its policies inadvertently (or advertently; there is a certain history here) destabilizes Guatemala or Nicaragua, the consequences for the United States are not terribly great. They are small countries and not directly on the U.S. border. But what about Mexico, with its 100 million people positioned right on the porous U.S. border? Such are the risks the United States now faces.

It is not that we Americans do not want democracy and honest elections in Mexico. But we need to temper our enthusiasm. The democracy agenda sometimes brings out the "true believer" mentality in us: such a strong desire to do well by our neighbors that we end up crushing them and destabilizing them in our embrace. The U.S. influence in Mexico is large and can easily be overwhelming. For by our insistence on absolutely fair elections rather than Mexico's usual ratificatory kind, by demanding transparency in place of Mexico's usual behind-the-scenes wheeling and dealing, by insisting on competition and pluralism in a system that has always been monist, by pushing for privatization in an economy that has always been mercantilist, by insisting on state downsizing in contrast with the usual Mexican practice of putting everyone on the public payroll, the United States could well destabilize Mexico. Again it is not that the goals of fair elections, transparency, pluralism, and privatization are not good ones but that we need to be careful about when, where, and how hard we push to achieve those goals. We should follow Mexico's lead rather than getting too far in front. Good sense and judgment should take priority over the purity of our intentions. For we need to remember where that road paved with good intentions can sometimes lead—and in a country where we can ill afford to make any mistakes.

Haiti

Haiti's situation is very different from Mexico's. Haiti has virtually no national institutions at all—certainly not those appropriate for or capable of holding together a functioning democracy. The policy dilemma in Haiti is therefore how to maintain at least the semblance of democracy when there are virtually no historical, cultural, economic, social, or political underpinnings for democracy.[5]

To begin, Haiti is by far the poorest country in Latin America. Its per capita income of less than $200 a year ranks Haiti with the least developed countries in the world. It has virtually no industry or manufacturing. Its meager agriculture is hampered by the fact that most of the country's meager topsoil has washed away over the past 200 years. It has no metals of significant value, no petroleum, almost no trees. Its un- and under-employment rate runs to 80–90 percent, by far the highest in Latin America. Strenuous U.S. efforts and guarantees have brought almost no investment to Haiti in recent years, either domestic or foreign. What little business, investment, and private sector existed in Haiti were largely eliminated by the U.S. embargo while the military was in power from 1991 to 1994. Most foreign aid experts in their private moments refer to the Haitian economy as "a basket case" or "hopeless." It is *conceivable* that democracy could be established in the context of such sheer poverty, but the odds are strongly against it.[6]

Nor has history been kind to Haiti–or prepared it for democracy. Haiti has *never* had democracy. The story is familiar. Haiti was a French sugar colony based on intense slave-plantation labor. In 1795 the slaves revolted, threw off their French masters, burned the plantations, and a decade later established the world's first black republic. But the country had few viable institutions, and the early republic quickly floundered. It reverted to more traditional subsistence agriculture; without institutions, it suffered one dictatorship after another. Haiti's plight was not helped by the fact that in the early nineteenth century the United States and most other countries still practiced slavery; they did not exactly welcome the independent black country into the family of nations. In the nineteenth and twentieth centuries short spells of disorder usually alternated with long spells of dictatorship. So if Haiti (and U.S. policy) now succeeds in consolidating democracy, it will be the first time ever. Again, the odds are long.

Culturally, Haiti is more akin to Africa than to the Hispanic- or English-speaking areas of North and South America. But here some further distinctions need to be drawn. Rural Haiti (about 70 percent of the population) retains many African customs and traditions, and many of these cultural traits are embedded in Haiti's institutions. Haiti is also about 70 to 80 percent illiterate, and the illiteracy corresponds with the rural population. This element largely lacks any training, experience, or education in democratic self-government. In the cities, however, the dominant culture tends to be a mixture of African and French–and now increasingly American. When this element talks of democracy, it largely has in mind a French, Rousseauian conception (centralized, organic, elite-led, top-down) and not the liberal, pluralist, *laissez faire* system of U.S.-style democracy.

Sociologically, Haiti is split between the poor, black, largely illiterate "peasants" of the countryside (the overwhelming majority of the population) and the wealthier, mulatto, Frenchified elites of the cities, primarily the capital of Port-au-Prince. Historically, the mulatto element has been dominant in business, banking, government, the bureaucracy, and social affairs, taking pains to keep the majority black population out of the national, social, economic, and political life. But when "Papa Doc" Duvalier came to power in 1957, he ruled for and in the name of the black population – the same constituency that overwhelmingly elected Jean Bertrand Aristide to the presidency in 1990. The mulatto elites, in turn, lacking a numerical majority, turned to the army to defend their interests and supported the 1991 coup that ousted Aristide. This racial *cum* social divide (not so much, as it is often portrayed, a divide between civilians and the military) remains bitter and rancorous, periodically tearing Haiti apart. Elections often help exacerbate these racial and class tensions, and Haiti has little middle class of any size. The prospects in this context for maintaining democracy there are not bright.

In terms of the institutions and infrastructure for democracy, Haiti again exhibits a vacuum. The country has *never* had a functioning system of political parties or competitive, balanced, pluralist interest groups. Anti-political party sentiment is strong; political parties are generally discredited, and it is no accident that Aristide's "Lavalas" is called a "movement" and not a "political party." Nor do government institutions, parliament, or the bureaucracy function as democratic institutions should. The long Duvalier dictatorship (father and son) prevented independent political parties, labor unions, peasant leagues, or interest groups of any kind from forming. Until the mid-1980s, the country entirely lacked what Alexis de Tocqueville called the "web of associability" necessary for democracy.[7]

At this point the argument gets trickier; one must be careful of the shoals of false data. Robert Maguire, an official of the Inter-American Foundation and an adviser on Haiti to the Clinton administration, has presented data that show "thousands" of community-based groups emerging in Haiti during the 1980s with "at least 2 million Haitians" (one-third the population) belonging to such groups.[8] These figures are enormously comforting to the Clinton administration's Haiti policy supporters. The data enable them to say that a nascent democracy functioning in Haiti during the 1980s was interrupted by military rule and only required Aristide to be restored for this democracy to flower again.

But most experts on Haiti are skeptical of these figures. The "thousands" of community-based groups mentioned by Maguire are, for the most part, paper organizations. Most were created and funded by USAID, the Catholic Church, and foreign nongovernmental organizations, but they lack indigenous roots, local leadership, and sufficient funds to be self-supporting. Almost all of them quickly faded away as soon as the coup occurred. In this sense they were like the constitutions and "single party systems" that seemed to offer some hope for democracy in the newly independent states of Africa in the early 1960s, but that proved to be purely paper facades that completely collapsed under the impact of a wave of military coups. If Maguire is right about this budding grassroots infrastructure in Haiti, then there is hope for Haitian democracy; but if the present analysis is correct, then Haiti still lacks sufficient organizational base on which democracy can be built. Most Haiti experts cannot find very much of the grassroots movement of which Maguire writes. One *wishes* the country did have such a web of associations, but of course policy cannot be based on wishful thinking or wishful sociology.

This analysis of Haiti adds up to a portrait of a country that would not seem to be particularly conducive of democracy. It lacks virtually all the requirements or prerequisites that would enable democracy to become established, let alone survive and thrive. The Clinton administration intervened in Haiti mainly at the behest of the Black Caucus in Congress, which was facing constituency demands and wanted Aristide restored, and the Florida congressional delegation, which wanted a stop to Haitians floating ashore on Florida beaches.[9] It had to justify the intervention in democracy terms both to satisfy these constituencies and because the restoration of democracy in Haiti gave it a legal and political "handle" to cut off Haitian emigration and return the Haitian "rafters" to their own country.

But no one should take seriously the administration's claim to having restored democracy to Haiti. "Democracy" of a sort continues in Haiti only because foreign military forces are still there keeping it in power, and the elections of 1995 that have been celebrated in some quarters represented only a rotation in the leadership (from Aristide to Rene Preval) of the dominant party, not a shift from a governing party to the opposition. Undoubtedly the human rights situation in Haiti is better than it was under the military dictatorship—again thanks mainly to the occupation military forces—but the economy remains a shambles. There is virtually no new investment, unemployment is as high as ever, and *none* of Haiti's intractable problems—few resources, far too many people—have been solved. The flow of emigres has been cut off, and Haiti no longer embarrasses the administration with dramatic and damaging headlines on our television screens every night. In these limited senses the administration's primary policy goals have been accomplished, but it is wrong and premature of Strobe Talbott and the administration to claim that Haiti is a resounding success for democracy and a morality-driven foreign policy.[10] A far longer term—50 years—is required before anyone can confidently assert that Haiti is safely in the democratic column.

Elections in this context have proven to be as much a polarizing and destabilizing influence as contributing to a hopefully future democracy. President Aristide was himself a polarizing and demagogic influence—and perhaps not even a democrat.[11] His candidacy and then presidency, in which he attempted to rule without and against the major power centers (the army and the mulatto elite) in Haiti, divided the country and left it even less institutionalized than before. The election of his successor Preval was terribly flawed, more a rotation among Lavalas leaders and a ratificatory election than one implying real choice. Indeed many democratically inclined Haitians prefer the calmer Preval to the rabble-rousing Aristide, hoping that the former stays in power and the latter remains out of the country. But Aristide has now returned and is setting his sights on the next election, which will likely be as divisive, destabilizing, and destructive of democracy as his earlier election. Haiti as well as democracy will again be the loser.

Haiti needs a period of calm, stable, centrist government. It will not have that with the volatile Aristide, who is certain to exacerbate already deep class and racial hatreds. In this sense and in this particular country, the elections strategy may have proved to be destructive of both democracy and the possibilities for Haitian development.

Peru and Guatemala

Peru presents a third and again very different case, one where, in my view, U.S. policy got it right for a change. The issue in Peru was President Alberto Fujimori's so-called *auto-golpe* or self-coup of 1992. When Fujimori was democratically elected to the presidency of Peru in 1990, he came to power in a nation with *almost* as many deep-seated problems as Haiti. Peru is one of the poorest and most fragmented countries in Latin America, and Fujimori had inherited a treasury from his predecessor, the demagogic Alan García, that was bankrupt. In addition, the vicious *Sendero Luminoso* and *Tupac Amaru* guerrilla movements, among the last left over from the Cold War era, were wreaking violence and destruction in the country, blowing up power grids, assassinating hundreds of farmers, tourists, and local officials, and seemingly closing in on the capital city. There were well-founded fears both in Peru and in the U.S. government that Peru and its democracy might collapse and disintegrate, and the guerrillas (akin to Cambodia's cruel and destructive Khmer Rouge) take over.[12]

In addition, Peru had emerged in the 1980s as *the* major source of drugs coming into the United States. Some of the drug-growing areas were quasi-autonomous, sapping the already meager strength of the Peruvian state; other areas were controlled by the guerrillas who were using the profits from the lucrative drug trade to finance their terrorist activities. On top of this, Peruvian society was disintegrating under the pressure of uncontrolled population growth, increased pauperization, rapid urbanization, and the massive, uncontrolled migration of the previously isolated and unintegrated majority Indian population into the capital city of Lima–migration accelerated partly by the destruction and violence Sendero Luminoso was wreaking in the countryside. Sendero's campaign of violence often precipitated indiscriminate counter-violence by the poorly trained police, army, and security forces, which made Peru a subject of frequent and negative human rights condemnations. From all angles it appeared that Peru's society, economy, and political system were falling apart, even that Peru as a national entity might cease to exist.[13]

The energetic, problem-solving Fujimori sought to address all these interrelated troubles, and in the first year of his presidency inflation went down, the economy began to recover, and the guerrillas were put on the defensive. He lacked a majority in the congress, however, and the nation's press, the opposition political parties, and established interests of various kinds seemed to be ganging up to defeat all his efforts at reform. Faced with these frustrations and the prospect of apparent national paralysis and breakdown, Fujimori determined to take drastic steps. In April 1992 he declared a state of siege, suspended the constitution, dissolved the congress, clamped down on the press and opposition activity, and determined to rule by decree-law. These steps were all taken legally, but they obviously were not very democratic.

The reaction to Fujimori's seizure of authoritarian power (albeit still within a Peruvian constitutional tradition) was swift and almost all of it condemnatory. Most of the criticism came from the international community; Peruvians themselves, who understood their own country's severe problems better than the outsiders, were less critical, and public opinion polls showed strong support for the president. Within days a storm of protest had blown up among the human rights community, religious groups, and within the U.S. Congress where these groups had access. They called for immediate condemnation of the steps Fujimori had taken, for sanctions to be imposed against Peru, for foreign aid and loans to be cut off, and for full democracy to be restored. Seldom in all this noise was the other side of the story presented: that Peru was in desperate straits and on the verge of disintegration, that drastic steps had to be taken, that strong presidential leadership was necessary to solve the many problems, and that the Peruvian constitution provided for the declaration of a state of emergency and rule by decree-law under the extraordinary and dangerous national situation then prevailing.

These differences were reflected in U.S. State Department policy debates as well, where one group wanted a strong condemnation of Fujimori while the other expressed understanding of his predicament and sought to emphasize the Fujimori administration's positive contributions in the counter-narcotics, economic development, and internal security areas rather than its anti-democratic steps. The result was an artful compromise: Fujimori's anti-democratic steps were condemned, but he was also praised for his other accomplishments. The condemnation was strongly worded, but did not contain strong or immediate economic or diplomatic sanctions. The United States suspended most foreign aid (small in any case) but continued humanitarian and counter-narcotics assistance. Instead of sanctions, Fujimori was obliged to appear before the Organization of American States where he was pressured to set forth a timetable for new elections, the ending of the emergency laws, and the restoration of constitutional rights. In these ways Fujimori was generally able to carry out the strong emergency steps that he believed necessary in Peru, and the rule of law was continued and democracy restored.

What accounts for the success of the Peru policy as contrasted with the many false starts and wrong directions in Haiti policy? Three factors may be briefly noted. First, Peru never became an intense domestic issue (no Black Caucus, no rafters, no Florida congressional delegation) the way Haiti did. Second, the Peru issue was addressed lower in the foreign policy bureaucracy, whereas Haiti became a matter of White House policymaking where (1) it was intensely politicized, and (2) there is no expertise on the issue. The third reason is the longtime expertise of persons at the State Department who have known Peru intimately and grasp the larger issues involved, whereas on Haiti neither of these two conditions prevailed. U.S. policy toward Peru was far more enlightened and balanced than policy toward Haiti.

THE CASE OF GUATEMALA was very similar to that of Peru's but in Guatemala both the policy and outcome were initially far less enlightened. However, in recent years Guatemala's situation appears to have improved.

Jorge Serrano had been inaugurated president of Guatemala in 1990, the first time an elected civilian had ever succeeded another in office in all of Guatemalan history. Serrano had been elected democratically in a competitive election; he was also the first Protestant to be elected to the presidency in *any* of the Central American countries.[14]

Although Guatemala's economy had improved under Serrano and there was progress in dealing with the guerrillas and curbing human rights abuses, the lot of the average citizen had not improved, and the Roman Catholic Church had lobbied actively against the Protestant president. In May 1993, hooded high school youths backed by their teachers staged street demonstrations to protest a rise in electricity rates and the requirement that they carry an identity card in order to continue free public bus service. There were bombings, tire burnings, and protests in which all groups with a grievance took to the streets. In response to the growing disorder, Serrano, with the backing of the military, dissolved the congress, sent the supreme court packing, and announced that he would rule by decree until a new constitution could be written. Serrano announced that he had taken these steps both to restore order and to root out corruption in congress and the courts, a charge not without foundation. These steps were similar to those taken earlier by Fujimori in Peru.

Immediately, a storm of protests blew up. The international outcry among the human rights groups, the religious lobbies, and the democracy/elections organizations was swift and loud. But in this case the internal Guatemalan opposition was also powerful. The domestic opposition to Serrano's self-coup included trade unions angry at his austerity program; human rights groups who wanted greater controls on the military; businessmen who feared U.S. economic sanctions; the Catholic Church, which resented and actively opposed the rise of Protestantism in Guatemala; and the U.S. embassy, which, more than in Peru, was under the spotlight of the democracy and human rights groups. In addition, not only did the State Department and the National Security Council have less expertise on Guatemala than on Peru but the strength and diversity of the opposition seemed to indicate that, unlike Peru, Serrano's *auto-golpe* enjoyed far less domestic popularity than did Fujimori's.

One *can*, however, make a strong case that Guatemala's problems were very similar to Peru's—widespread poverty and illiteracy, an unassimilated Indian population, drugs, disorder, corruption, guerrilla movements, national paralysis—and required a strong hand at the helm. But in the face of the widespread opposition, as well as the threat of economic and military aid cutoffs, both domestic and foreign, the Guatemalan armed forces, which had initially backed Serrano, began to have second thoughts. It negotiated a settlement under which Serrano was forced to leave office. Vice President Gustavo Espina would take over until congress could designate a successor, and congress would purge *itself* (!) of corruption. However, when Espina declared he was the legitimate constitutional successor and the military prepared to back him, a new round of protests began, led by the same groups that had opposed the original self-coup, including Rigoberta Menchu, the Marxist-spouting indigenous icon whose ghost-written (by Regis Debray's wife) book had garnered her a Nobel prize and made her the only Guatemalan whom uninformed outsiders could identify.

To end the turmoil, the opposition coalition, backed by the military, submitted a list of three presidential nominees to the congress, which then chose Ramiro de Leon Carpio as president. De Leon had been Guatemala's human rights prosecutor and was known as a romantic, somewhat naive, idealist. The fact that he was chosen by the congress rather than by the people cast doubts on his democratic legitimacy. He added further to his difficulties by sacking the military high command, thus antagonizing the most powerful element in Guatemalan politics. Within months the consensus that had agreed on Serrano's departure and the elevation of de Leon to the presidency had collapsed, leaving Guatemala as divided and polarized as ever.

Guatemala is one of those countries whose problems are all but insurmountable. If rated on a scale, Guatemala would be somewhat better off than Haiti but somewhat worse off (fewer resources but many of the same problems) than Peru. It is a deeply riven society whose political system has been going through wildly oscillating swings of the pendulum ever since the Guatemalan revolution of 1944 and the U.S. intervention of 1954. In Guatemala's unfortunate circumstances, where strong presidential leadership is necessary just to hold the country together, we should not realistically expect an absolutely pristine form of democracy to operate. Yet by insisting on democracy in its purest form in the case of the Serrano *auto-golpe*, both Guatemalan opposition groups and U.S. policy produced a situation where an elected and constitutional president was ousted, and a romantic and ineffective president who lacked democratic legitimacy was installed in his place. Guatemala polarized and continued to spiral downhill. Surely the compromise that was reached in the case of Fujimori in Peru is to be preferred to the severe damage that a "purer" policy wreaked on Guatemala.

Venezuela

Venezuela is often cited as a political and economic success story with a long and continuous (since 1958) record of democracy and, until recently, the highest per capita income in Latin America. Faced with difficult policy issues in Peru and other Latin American countries, U.S. policymakers often gazed wistfully at Venezuela, as they did at Costa Rica during the great Central America policy "wars" (there is no other term) of the 1980s. They wonder why the other countries cannot be as peaceful, prosperous, and democratic as these two. But of course Venezuela, like Costa Rica, is a unique case with its own characteristics; neither the Venezuelan nor the Costa Rican "model" can be simply picked up and transported to some other country where the history, resources, and institutions are quite different.

To begin, Venezuela almost literally floats on oil, which has helped finance its modernization process. Now it is *possible* for a comparatively poor country (Costa Rica but not Haiti) to become democratic, but the odds clearly improve, as in Venezuela, when there is great natural wealth. In Venezuela, too, class and racial lines are not so sharply or rigidly drawn as in other Latin American countries, which helps provide for a more egalitarian society. Moreover, Venezuela's cosmopolitan, well-educated citizenry provides large pools of skilled, well-trained technicians, managers, and administrators who can ably fill posts in government as well as the private sector. In addition, Venezuela is a well-institutionalized country with well-organized political parties, trade unions, business groups, and civic associations.[15]

In recent years, however, Venezuela has developed grave trouble. Oil prices were depressed for several years in the 1980s, which sent the economy into a tailspin and resulted in a 25 percent decrease in GNP. Corruption and patronage have flourished in a regime that has a large state sector still organized on a patrimonialist basis. The long-term economic downturn has increased class tensions, violence, and a sense of malaise. Political institutions, among the most democratic in Latin America in the 1960s and early 1970s, have since become ossified, hardened, and corrupt. Whereas in much of Latin America, corporatism was associated with authoritarian regimes, in Venezuela the various corporate groups (military, unions, farmers, business, public corporations) have all hived off sectors of, or insinuated themselves into, the political parties as well as the state sector, milking off contracts, patronage, sinecures, entitlements, special privileges, and graft on a grand scale. Venezuela presents the interesting case of widespread corporatist practices within a multiparty and democratic system.[16]

Recently the tensions generated by long-term economic decline, mounting social problems, and political sclerosis have come dramatically to the surface. In 1989 Venezuela experienced violent "food riots" when urban slum-dwellers spilled out of their *barrios* and took over, trashed, and looted private groceries and other stores. The police then responded with their own violence, but the takeovers continue. Fearing still greater crime and violence and distrustful of the ability of public authorities to deal with it, middle- and upper-class neighborhoods in and around Caracas have created high walls and employed large private security agencies to police the entrances to their complexes. In 1992 two coup attempts were made that generated considerable public sympathy and came within a whisker of succeeding. The following year the corrupt but populist president Carlos Andres Pérez was "suspended" from office on the grounds of misusing government funds. Venezuela appeared to be unraveling; the most developed democracy in Latin America seemed to be coming apart at the seams.[17]

The president elected in 1994, Rafael Caldera, had served in the presidency before (1969–1974) and was thus both a senior statesman and deemed to be uncorruptible. He had been a Christian-Democrat and an old-fashioned Catholic-corporatist whose formative ideas dated to the 1930s. He believed in the organic unity of society, centralization, the founding of society on its "natural" corporatist basis (families, parishes, etc.), a guiding and directing role by the state in economic matters, and the harmony of business and labor. Not only did U.S. policymakers, who have been educated to think of Latin American politics as a constant struggle between authoritarianism and democracy, fail to understand any of Caldera's corporatist background, but they also pushed him to adopt the neoliberal economic package (state-downsizing, open markets, austerity, privatization) for which Caldera had little understanding or sympathy. He believed the neoliberal formula (part of the "Washington consensus" of the early 1990s) might produce national disintegration, renewed riots and coup attempts, a repeat of the debacle that resulted in his predecessor's ouster, and a situation as in Mexico in 1994 and continuing today where the peso devaluation triggered a devastating economic and political crisis. Caldera much preferred a mercantilist and corporatist approach, but under pressure from the United States and the international lending agencies as well as a collapsing domestic economy, he gradually, reluctantly, and in piecemeal fashion began to implement the neoliberal agenda.

In the United States, politicians seem hardly able even to *begin* to reform the ailing, nearly bankrupt Medicare, Medicaid, and Social Security systems; why should Americans expect democratic politicians in a far poorer and politically precarious country like Venezuela to implement strict austerity programs that we can scarcely talk about as yet? In addition the poll data we have for Venezuela (and for other Latin American countries) is really quite striking, indicating that Caldera is far closer to the mainstreams of Venezuelan public opinion than are the Americans and international banking officials who presume to tell him how to govern.[18]

For example, only 60 percent of Venezuelans (down from 80 percent a decade ago) believe that democracy is preferable to any other alternatives. Fully 40 percent of Venezuelans now say that "it depends on the circumstances"—not exactly a ringing endorsement of democracy. In addition, some 65 percent of Venezuelans (more than those who call democracy preferable to any other system) prefer "strong government"—a strong statist and mercantilist role. Venezuelans have very little faith in what we think of as "civil society" or the supporting pluralism of institutions of a democratic society: less than a quarter of the population supports political parties (any party), labor unions, or the congress. At the same time Venezuelans are intensely nationalistic; they not only resent International Monetary Fund, World Bank, and U.S. embassy intervention in their internal affairs but—again with Mexico clearly in mind—think the prescriptions by these outside forces are downright harmful to their economy and society.

Clearly then the Venezuelans prefer a democratic and elected government but one that is strong, centralized, corporatist, mercantilist, and nationalist. And if one thinks about it for a moment, that is precisely the kind of regime that Caldera personifies—a regime that U.S. policy has been roundly criticizing and urging to take a neoliberal direction. But why should Caldera, any more than American politicians, go in a direction that his countrymen clearly do not wish to go; and why should we in the United States expect a Venezuelan politician to commit political suicide when we do not have the same expectations of our own political leaders?

The U.S. policy problem in Venezuela, therefore, differs

from the previous cases. It is not that Venezuela does not want or is unsuited for democracy and elections; in fact, Venezuelan democracy and elections may be as healthy and vigorous—certainly as judged by electoral turnout—as our own. Instead, the problem is an almost complete lack of understanding in the United States of what Venezuela means by democracy, a lack of comprehension that there may be other forms of democracy (in this case, corporatist and Rousseauian) from our own, a lack of empathy for Venezuelan realities and ways of doing things, and a U.S. insistence on pushing Venezuela in a direction on economic policy that it clearly does not want to—and perhaps cannot, given the prevailing public opinion—go. It is not that Venezuela's mercantilism is preferable, only that U.S. pressure to push reform too quickly may produce destabilization.

The Dominican Republic

The Dominican Republic shares the island of Hispaniola with much poorer Haiti. The Dominican Republic occupies two-thirds of the territory on Hispaniola, but Haiti has long had two-thirds of the people and is far more crowded demographically. And although Haiti was a French colony, the Dominican Republic was Spanish and retains pride in its Hispanic institutions. Also, with a per-capita income of about $1,000 to $1,200 per year, the Dominican Republic is about five times wealthier than Haiti.[19]

Since the mid-1960s—following a long history of instability and dictatorship, an aborted attempt at democracy under Juan Bosch, and revolution, civil war, and U.S. military intervention in 1965—the Dominican Republic has been largely dominated by one man—Joaquín Balaguer. Except for the interlude from 1978 to 1986, Balaguer had been in power for 22 of the 30 years between 1966 and 1996. Everyone agrees that Balaguer was a shrewd, clever, manipulative, Machiavellian politician of the first order. Although not a bloody totalitarian or human rights abuser on the scale of other recent authoritarian regimes in Latin America, Balaguer nevertheless sometimes employed arbitrary methods, used patronage extensively, and was not a great believer in liberalism and democracy. Like Rafael Caldera in Venezuela, Balaguer had been shaped politically during his formative years, the 1930s, by the *etatist*, Catholic-corporatist, and organicist political beliefs prevalent in Europe and Latin America at that time.

Between 1966 and 1996 the Dominican Republic has held regular presidential elections at four-year intervals. Balaguer won the 1966 and 1986 elections in fair, competitive elections; in 1970 and 1974 he won with no or only token opposition, his main competition complaining it was prevented from campaigning effectively. In 1978 the United States intervened diplomatically to ensure a democratic outcome, which the opposition won; and in 1982 the main opposition, the Dominican Revolutionary Party or PRD, won again. But in 1990 and then again in 1994 there were widespread charges that Balaguer had won by fraud, using various techniques but mainly relying on the method of eliminating likely opposition voters from the official voting lists and thus preventing them from voting.[20]

The uproar following the 1994 election was particularly strong, involving both domestic foes of Balaguer and the international election observer teams present in the country for the voting. The opposition was never able to produce a "smoking gun" or definitive proof that Balaguer and his followers had employed fraud; nevertheless, circumstantial evidence abounded, and the computer programs employed to register voters and count the votes pointed toward electoral manipulation. Most independent observers of the election were convinced that some degree of fraud had been used. Whether the *extent* of the fraud was sufficient to give the election to the opposition PRD, however, remained open to question. For Balaguer, as a father figure and patronage politician, also had undoubtedly strong political support, and the extent of the alleged fraud was only marginally greater than the number of votes separating the two leading candidates.

In the Dominican Republic, the 1994 electoral process and results triggered an upheaval among certain sectors of the usually quiescent population who were determined either to annul the election or to make certain the next election was not similarly marred by fraud. Members of the Roman Catholic Church, labor leaders, opposition party officials, journalists, and academics joined forces both to pressure the government to instigate electoral reforms and/or to make sure that Balaguer did not run again.

The Clinton administration and the U.S. government also entered the dispute. Some among the more ideologically oriented of the Clinton administration appointees wished to use U.S. pressure to *force* Balaguer from power and to install in the Dominican presidency the more ideologically compatible opposition candidate, José Francisco Peña Gómez, who was also black. They pushed this agenda despite the fact that they could not actually prove fraud or that there were even enough fraudulent votes to tip the election to Peña.

Others in the U.S. government opposed this option, mainly for two reasons. First, they argued that the United States had *many* interests in the Dominican Republic besides elections and that policy should not be determined by simply one facet of what was a multiple set of interests. A second and even more important factor at the time was U.S. policy toward neighboring Haiti. The United States at this point was engaged in a strenuous, White House–level, high-stakes political effort to pressure the Haitian military to step aside and to restore Aristide to power. It needed Dominican cooperation along their common border to help enforce the economic blockade of Haiti, to allow U.S. military forces to be stationed in the Dominican Republic, and to have Dominican cooperation in handling Haitian refugees whom the United States wanted to stop coming to the United States itself. None of these objectives would be served by a change of government or instability in the neighboring Dominican Republic. In this case, then, after an intense internal political battle, the Clinton administration ideologues were reined in and a more pragmatic policy employed.

The resulting policy compromise included the following elements: Balaguer would be acknowledged as the winner of the 1994 election (thus providing for continuity of government and of U.S. policy vis-à-vis Haiti), but his term would be limited to two years instead of the usual four (thus satisfying the opposition). Moreover, Balaguer would not be allowed to be a candidate for reelection in 1996, so that his era would definitively come to an end. In addition, the United States extracted concessions that would enable the electoral machinery and computers to be reformed and updated, a new electoral commission to be appointed, and more honest vote-counting procedures to be put in place. USAID then moved forcefully to support emerging Dominican civil society groups to *ensure* that Balaguer would live up to his promise not to seek reelection. This compromise satisfied the several *American* policy positions involved, but it still left President Balaguer ou of the picture; he was apparently brought around by the assurance he could take the presidential oath once again (albeit limited to two years and no reelection) in return for his greater cooperation on the Haiti issue.

This artful and pragmatic compromise—in many ways comparable to the one reached over Fujimori in Peru, but very different from the strongly ideological policy stands taken on Haiti and Guatemala—seems both reasonable and realistic. Both democracy *and* stability were preserved. Both change *and* continuity were ensured. Balaguer got his new term in office (at least for two years), and the opposition got a new and stronger chance (with AID support and new electoral machinery) at replacing him, which occurred in 1996 with the election of Leonel Fernández. U.S. policy in favor of democracy was continued and even enhanced (through the AID initiatives), while the larger and many-faceted U.S. interests in the Dominican Republic and, more importantly, in Haiti were also protected.

It would have been admirable if the motive for this compromise had been a genuine understanding of Dominican-style democracy and not the already flawed Haiti policy. As in Caldera's Venezuela, the Dominican conception of democracy involves strongly mercantilist, patrimonialist, statist, centralist, corporatist, and organicist conceptions and not so much American-style liberalism and pluralism; the Dominican conception is Rousseauian rather than Lockean or Madisonian. The best and most thorough public opinion survey ever done in the Dominican Republic, as in virtually all of the Latin American countries, shows a decided preference for strong government along with democracy, for statism and mercantilism over neoliberalism, for paternalistic leadership over separation of powers.[21] It would be nice to report that U.S. policymakers understood the currents underlying Latin American democracy on *their* terms rather than through the rose-colored lenses of U.S. political institutions and practices.

Nevertheless this compromise and the pragmatism shown in reaching it seem viable. It accomplished *most* of our objectives without the negative implications of the other more ideological policy options considered. The U.S. officials involved in the compromise showed a maturity, balance, sophistication, and understanding of Dominican realities not always present in U.S. policy. The policy could have been even better if the United States had exhibited a deeper comprehension of what the Dominican Republic means and implies by democracy, how that differs from the U.S. conception, and what the policy implications of these differences are.

4

Conclusion and
Policy Recommendations

At the close of 1996, more of the world's countries were free and democratic than ever before. The annual Freedom House survey indicates that a majority of the world's population now lives under democratic rule. In a survey of 191 countries, Freedom House lists 79 as free and able to enjoy a broad range of civil and political rights and an additional 59 countries as "partly free" and under some constraints on basic rights. Free nations now constitute 1.25 billion people or 21.7 percent of the world's population of 5.77 billion, while 2.26 billion people accounting for 39.2 percent of the world's population are in the partly free category. The totals of free and partly free nations include 138 countries, 3.51 billion people, or 60.9 percent of the world's total.[1]

Especially interesting for the purposes of this study was Freedom House's report of an all-time high of 118 electoral democracies in the world. The trend toward electoral democracy was particularly strong in Latin America, Asia's Pacific Rim, Eastern and Central Europe, and Russia and the countries of the former Soviet Union. The trend was weakest in Africa and the Islamic countries. Particularly significant for our analysis was Freedom House's finding that, of the 118 "electoral democracies" in the world, one-third of them still represented countries that were only partly free or incompletely democratic. It is these countries that constitute the bulk of the countries examined in this analysis.

The advance of freedom and democracy in the world is one of the great transformations of the late twentieth century, and all Americans have reason to be justly proud of the accomplishments these trends represent. But the Freedom House surveys, welcome as they are, and much policy analysis of these same themes gloss over and obscure important issues at the heart of this volume. First, the surveys ignore the fact that such terms as "free" and "democratic" often mean different things or—even if we agree on such fundamentals as competitive elections, constitutionalism, and basic rights—carry different shadings and implications in different countries. Second, Freedom House's three-part categorization—Free, Partly Free, Not Free—or our even more familiar dichotomy between democratic and authoritarian, ignore the complex mixed forms, overlaps, hybrids, and crazy-quilt patterns that characterize many countries. And third, such surveys provide no guidelines for understanding the complex processes and dynamics of moving from one category to the next—and sometimes back again. In fact, the process of transitioning from authoritarianism (Left or Right) to democracy should be conceptualized as involving not two or three categories but a continuum or spectrum along which *all countries* are, so to speak, strung out.

Now, most of us have little trouble recognizing at one end of this spectrum obviously free and democratic regimes. We know them when we see them. At the same time, most of us instinctively know when we are dealing with or living under an authoritarian or Not Free regime. These two types of regimes at both ends of the spectrum are easily recognizable, and we generally have tried and true ways of dealing with them in a policy sense. But the mixed, overlapping, hybrid cases are hardest to categorize. These regimes are also often the ones *in transition* from one category to another. They are also the ones that attract the most attention or cause the most difficulty for policymakers. Surveys such as Freedom House's fail to provide us with a conceptual framework for analyzing these complex and mixed cases at the heart of the policy dilemmas analyzed in this study.

THREE MAIN THEMES have emerged from this analysis. The first, elaborated below, is that democracy may mean different things or take different forms in different countries and culture areas. The second is that the chances of democracy's succeeding are better in some countries than others, depending on such factors as history, political culture, level of socioeconomic development, and institutional infrastructure. The third finding is that the instruments of U.S. democracy initiatives and a heavy-handed, impatient, ethnocentric U.S. policy often work at cross-purposes with the efforts to establish viable democratic countries and are thus often self-defeating. These three findings all carry important implications both for the advance of democracy and for U.S. policy.

Democracy, as seen earlier in this analysis, comes in many different forms and many different institutional and sociological arrangements. Even beginning students in Comparative Politics learn that democracy in Great Britain is very different from democracy in the United States; democracy in France is very different from either of the previous two and quite different from democracy in Germany. When the analysis is extended to include other European countries, clearly democracy in Scandinavia is very different from democracy in Italy, while democracy in Spain is quite different from democracy in any of the others. Even Spain and Portugal, superficially similar and with both having embarked on democracy in the mid-1970s, represent quite different forms of democracy.

Although Americans recognize and accept these differences among democracies in Europe, we have been less willing to accept other forms and definitions of democracy outside Europe. We may concede that Japan and India are democracies, for example, but in the former case we are not quite sure if it is "fully" democratic while in the latter we worry that it may not have the socioeconomic underpinnings to support democracy. These sentiments are even more pronounced with regard to new democracies in Russia, the Islamic countries, Eastern Europe, Asia, Africa, and Latin America. The questions are mainly three: (1) Do they have the political culture, the values and beliefs of a civic and civil society conducive to democracy? (2) Do they have the socioeconomic underpinnings to support democracy? (3) Are they fully democratic or only partially so? These questions have gained added currency as the United States launched over the past two decades a pro-democracy foreign policy, as more countries in fact became democratic, and as the end of the Cold War freed up policy to concentrate more on the democracy agenda.

The end of the Cold War means that the major strategic threat of the past 40 years—the Soviet Union and its empire—is gone. True, the United States must still be concerned with rogue states and numerous problems of drug-trafficking, ungovernability, civil strife, ethnic conflict, and terrorism (on a lesser scale); but none of these—or even all of them combined—constitutes the severe and massive threat of annihilation that the Soviet Union did for all those decades. Without such a strong external threat, the United States can now afford to emphasize the democracy/human rights issue more than before. Earlier, the United States could enter into partnerships or alliances with nondemocratic states (Spain, China, South Korea, for example) and justify these in the name of the Cold War; but now, without such a severe threat, alliances with such regimes—and maybe even nondemocratic regimes themselves—cannot be tolerated any more. One cannot imagine that the current great debate over human rights in China, for example, could have occurred with the same intensity while China was strategically useful as a check on the Soviet Union.

Democracy is thus now at or near the top of U.S. foreign policy priorities. We have always, as a moralistic and missionary nation with a strong sense of American exceptionalism, valued democracy and often acted on its behalf, but now we can afford, in the absence of serious threats that argue for a national interest-based strategy, to elevate democracy in importance as a foreign policy objective. In fact, both public opinion and our own history and values as a nation dictate that the cause of democracy be an American priority. Some even wish to elevate it into being *the* number one and *virtually only* priority.

Although Americans welcome the global spread of democracy, the new democratic emphasis in U.S. foreign policy, and the current opportunity to give higher priority to democracy, we need to recognize the pitfalls in this policy as well. Greater democracy is not always an unmixed blessing. Some countries may not want it, or want it all that badly, or want it in our precise form; and in several of the cases analyzed here democracy has proved or has the potential to prove destructive of both stability and economic growth, *and* American interests. These reservations about the democracy agenda, again, apply particularly in the countries that are mixed cases, or that are in transition–usually incomplete–from one form to another. So let us indeed celebrate the expansion of democracy in the world, meanwhile recognizing the policy traps and pitfalls present especially in the mixed and transitional cases where the guidelines for policymakers are often unclear.

THE PATH TO DEMOCRACY is neither inevitable nor unilinear. There are often many interruptions, even reversals, along the way. Here are some policy guidelines:

First, Americans must recognize that there are many different definitions of democracy.[2] I am not here talking of the transparent perversions of democracy by the so-called people's republics (the few that are left) or their counterparts on the Right, but of genuine, historically and culturally based differences over democracy's precise forms, meanings, and institutions. In some parts of Asia, for example, history and the Confucian tradition point to a form of democracy that is more consensus-based and less confrontational than the West's; in Latin America, the Thomistic and Rousseauian (along with the U.S.) influences point to a type of democracy that is both paternalistic, centralized, organic, and corporatist, *and* based on liberal Lockean principles. These differences should not overconcern us in a policy sense, and we should be careful not to push these countries too hard or too fast in the direction of an inappropriate (for them) U.S.-style democracy lest we destabilize them–with disastrous policy consequences–in the process. At the same time, we should remain open as to whether the new kinds of indigenous-based institutions (greater consultations between rulers and ruled in the Islamic states, ethnically based representation and delivery of social services in Africa) might not be valuable *first steps* on the *route* to

democracy. Rather than simply using the too-simple democracy/
authoritarianism or free/not free categorizations, policy needs to
recognize many intermediary and transitional stages. Meanwhile,
without destabilizing them as some Western programs have unfortunately done in the past, we can continue *nudging* these regimes toward greater democracy.

Second, and implied in the above, Americans should recognize various mixed, qualified, and hybrid forms of democracy—
"democracy with adjectives" as it is sometimes called. These include various kinds of paternalistic, controlled, partial, or tutelary
democracies. Although obviously not full or complete democracies, they are often several steps above authoritarianism or totalitarianism. At certain early stages in their development, such partial forms of democracy may be about all that some emerging
countries—often weakly institutionalized and lacking a strong
socioeconomic infrastructure—can bear. We should not try to
push these countries too far toward a type of advanced democracy
that their own, often incomplete institutions and level of social
and economic development cannot support; at the same time,
we should not settle for second-best solutions when the conditions are appropriate to again nudge that country toward greater
democracy.

A third and related point is the need to recognize limits.
Where is Western-style democracy realistically possible and where
is it not? In South Africa, with its wealth, resources, literacy, and
high living standards, democracy has good possibilities, but in
most of the poorer areas of Africa democracy faces a long, uphill
battle. Much of Latin America, more developed than Africa on a
variety of indices, has made a successful transition to and even
consolidated democracy over the past two decades, but we
should recognize that in far poorer and less institutionalized
countries such as Haiti, democracy's possibilities are slim and
should not be oversold. Either the Clinton administration erred
in thinking of Haiti as up to the level of the rest of Latin America
in its measures of socioeconomic development and therefore
ready for democracy; or, as Strobe Talbott himself (one of the
architects of the Haiti policy) tells it, he was told by a Venezuelan
leader that if democracy did not survive in Haiti, democracy

would be in trouble *everywhere* in Latin America.[3] Nothing could be farther from the truth: Haiti is way below the socioeconomic level of the rest of Latin America, and none of the countries of the area believes that what happens in Haiti will affect their democracies. Talbott, who knows little about Latin America, was either misled or sold a bill of goods by his Venezuelan friend.

Democracy can obviously emerge in cultures other than Western ones, and as noted no necessary causal relationship exists between socioeconomic levels and democracy. Clearly, however, some cultures such as Islam have not been particularly hospitable to democracy. At the same time, although there is no causal relation between national wealth and democracy, there *are* strong correlations. The facts are that democracy is far more likely to be found in literate, affluent, and market-oriented societies while less-developed countries have a much harder time establishing and maintaining democracy. As Sophie Tucker said about her own life—and *apropos* of democracy as well—"I've been rich and I've been poor. Rich is better."

A fourth point has to do with the distinction between realism and idealism in foreign policy. Historically the pursuit of democracy and human rights has been closely identified with the idealistic position, as in the Carter administration, and has often been denigrated by the more hard-headed realists. But recall how under Reagan this historic distinction began to be bridged: the pursuit of democracy and human rights was turned into a hard-headed, eminently realistic program to salvage our foreign policy chestnuts in El Salvador and as an instrument to help delegitimize and undermine communist regimes in the Soviet Union and Eastern Europe. President Bush as an experienced foreign policy practitioner also recognized how to employ a set of instruments identified with idealism (democracy, human rights) to secure hard-headed national-interest objectives.

However, the Clinton administration came into office either with retread officials from the Carter administration seeking to vindicate themselves for past policy misdirections (Christopher, Lake), rejecting in knee-jerk fashion and therefore failing to understand that they might have learned something from the policies of the intervening Republican administrations, or filled with such new and naive enthusiasms ("aggressive multilateralism," "enlargement") that they verged on a new romanticism. That is how the administration during its first two years stumbled into such foreign policy disasters as "nation-building" in Somalia (for which we have almost no experience or knowledge), "restoring democracy to restore), and "peacekeeping" in Bosnia (when, in fact, there was precious little peace to keep). By 1996 the administration had begun to appear more pragmatic and realistic administration had begun to appear more pragmatic and realistic ("America must lead"), but the idealistic urge unleavened by realism periodically still flares into public view. Democracy and human rights need to be supported, of course, but such enthusiasms need to be tempered, as in Peru and the Dominican Republic, by considerations of where and when these policies can be reasonably pursued and where they are likely to succeed in ways that also serve the national interest.

A fifth and related point has to do with the conflict between the generally older veterans who inhabit any administration and the usually younger ideologues who often dominate discussion at the beginning of a new presidency. The young ideologues are often fire-breathers, shaped by a divisive campaign and absolutely convinced that they have a monopoly on truth. They were usually advance persons or luggage carriers during the campaign but now have high administration positions, power, and the certainty of their convictions. That was clearly the situation in the Dominican case examined here where the young administration ideologues at State, the NSC, and the OAS tried to manipulate Balaguer out of office and shoehorn Peña Gómez into it, potentially with disastrous consequences. But in that case, the more prudent pragmatists triumphed in the end and a compromise was reached. In general, it often takes the foreign policy professionals about two years to recapture policy from the ideologues who accompany a new president into office.[4] Note that this—two years—was about the time period that it took for the Clinton administration to recover its moorings and move toward more centrist foreign policy (and other) positions.

Sixth, although the end of the Cold War enables the United States to emphasize the democracy concerns it prizes, still these are *not the only* issues in U.S. foreign policy, and they must be weighed against other interests. The United States has vast economic, political, diplomatic, and strategic interests around the globe as well as democracy ones. Examples abound even in this post–Cold War world that is ripe for more democracy. In Saudi Arabia, stability and petroleum interests outweigh U.S. interests in democracy; in Algeria (following the French lead) the U.S. desire to avoid an Islamic fundamentalist regime in power overrode democracy interests; in the Dominican Republic, the need for regional stability and help with the Haiti problem eventually forced a compromise on the democracy issue. In China the issues of trade, the sale of weapons of mass destruction, an emerging regional hegemon, and influence over North Korea seem at least as important as advancing democracy and human rights. In Russia, similarly, other issues—the threat of uncontrolled nuclear weapons, worry about a reconstituted Russian threat, and fear about the consequences of further disintegration for that immense region and its neighbors—are just as important. Fortunately the Russian case has proven again the wisdom of trying to use what Americans often think of as an idealistic instrument (democracy) to secure very hard-headed and realistic goals (stability, central control of nuclear weapons).

An exceedingly important case in this respect is Mexico. Mexico is the last country in the world the United States would want to see destabilized, yet the possibilities of that happening—and of the United States inadvertently and with the best of intentions assisting that process by pushing too hard and too fast on the democracy/elections/free market agenda—are very real. It is not necessarily that experienced policymakers will pressure Mexico too hard and thus add to the disintegrative forces already present in the country—although that may happen, too, and may have been a factor in the 1994 peso crisis. It is that the sheer proximity, interconnectedness (on thousands of fronts), and influence of U.S. culture, prosperity, and power may overwhelm Mexico and cause it to unravel. The consequences of that eventuality are so immense that we would rather not even contemplate them. By following prudent policies, the United States can strengthen Mexico economically and politically, but a too rapid or too heavy-handed effort at change could unleash its disintegrative forces.

Finally, the seventh point is the close relationship between domestic and foreign policy. It is now generally understood, particularly with the end of the Cold War, that foreign policy and domestic policy have come closer together, that politics no longer stops at the water's edge.[5] The increased connectedness of foreign and domestic policy is most obvious in such areas as trade, drugs, and immigration. But to say analytically that foreign and domestic policy have become increasingly intertwined is far different from the *celebration* of that fact or the blatant turning over of entire areas of foreign policy to domestic political interests: Haiti policy to the Florida congressional delegation and the Black Caucus, Cuba policy to the Cuban exile community, environmental policy to the environmental lobbyists, the Commerce Department to business groups, family planning policy to the population groups, and democracy policy to the democracy/human rights ideologues and absolutists. It is unconscionable, as Mr. Clinton perhaps even more than other recent presidents has done, to repeat what all foreign policy analysts know about the increasing links between foreign and domestic policy, but then to use that analytical point as a rationalization for handing out whole realms of policy to interested groups for blatantly domestic political purposes. Foreign policy should not and cannot be treated like state highway contracts and other patronage goodies to be doled out to favored groups in return for political support and campaign contributions. That is a formula for disaster.

ABOVE ALL, THEN, THIS IS A PLEA for balance, prudence, realism, good sense, pragmatism, and compromise in U.S. efforts to promote democracy abroad. Because of low levels of socioeconomic development, political cultures that may be unsupportive of democratic values, and the absence of institutional infrastructure, there are some countries in which democracy has very slim possibilities of succeeding. And because it is far better in a policy sense to support winners than losers, the United States needs to be very wary of trying to create or construct democracy in places where the odds are so long. We need also to recognize that many countries mean something different by democracy than we do, and we need to be not just aware of these differences but also to recognize that they often cannot and will not produce exact replicas of our institutions. Then too, there are some countries (Saudi Arabia, Kuwait) where we had probably better not talk (publicly) about democracy for fear of jeopardizing even more crucial interests—oil and thus the U.S. economy; and other countries (China) where democracy/human rights issues need to be balanced against other important (political, economic, strategic) U.S. interests. Another fear is that democracy as in Algeria or even Russia may encourage or even bring to power nativist political movements hostile to the United States and the West in general.

A particularly worrisome aspect at present is that, in the name of democracy and with the best of intentions, U.S. enthusiasms for democracy could inadvertently destabilize a number of countries that are the last countries we should want to see unstable. Mexico and Russia come quickly to mind but there are others as well. Democratization, it must be remembered, is not always a peaceful, clean, and antiseptic process (witness Bosnia), but may instead involve wrenching transformations, profound disruptions, and frequent bloodshed. The danger is that old institutions and ways of doing things could be destroyed before new ones have been consolidated, producing a vacuum and paving the way for disintegration and chaos—the very dangers U.S. policy and its democracy initiatives were designed to prevent.

Proceeding too slowly on the democratization front is likely to result in too little progress toward democracy, but pushing too hard and too fast can be equally disastrous. U.S. leadership in this area is like a bus driver: if the bus proceeds too slowly, the passengers may well get off and take another form of transportation; but a speeding bus could cause a wreck that ruins all hopes. U.S. policy should seek to promote democracy, therefore, where and when it can, but also needs to reign in the "true believers" who would make the democracy agenda into a missionary crusade involving unacceptable degrees of ethnocentrism, interference in the internal affairs of other nations, and downright destructive behavior that might well produce not democracy but destabilization of countries we cannot afford to see destabilized. As often is the case, a prudent, centrist, and politically sensitive policy is the one that will best serve U.S. interests *and* the cause of democracy.

Notes

Chapter 1

1. The main literature includes Louis Hartz, *The Liberal Tradition in America* (New York: Harcourt Brace, 1955); Larry Diamond, *Promoting Democracy in the 1990s* (Washington, D.C.: Carnegie Commission, 1995); S. M. Lipset, *American Exceptionalism: A Double-Edged Sword* (New York: W. W. Norton, 1996); Abraham F. Lowenthal, ed., *Exporting Democracy: The United States and Latin America* (Baltimore: Johns Hopkins University Press, 1991); Joshua Muravchik, *Exporting Democracy: Fulfilling America's Destiny* (Washington, D.C.: AEI Press, 1991); and Tony Smith, *America's Mission: The United States and the Worldwide Struggle for Democracy in the Twentieth Century* (Princeton, N.J.: Princeton University Press, 1994).

2. Kissinger began as an apostle of *realpolitik*; it was his service as chair of the National Bipartisan Commission on Central America that led him to acknowledge the importance of democracy and human rights concerns as essential to successful U.S. foreign policy; see *Report of the President's National Bipartisan Commission on Central America* (New York: Macmillan, 1984).

3. See the general treatment as well as individual country treatments in Daniel Pipes and Adam Garfinkle, eds., *Friendly Tyrants: An American Dilemma* (New York: Doubleday, 1991).

4. Carl Bernstein and Marco Politi, *His Holiness: John Paul II and the Hidden History of Our Time* (New York: Doubleday, 1996).

5. Tamar Jacoby, "The Reagan Turnabout on Human Rights," *Foreign Affairs* (Summer 1986): 1066–1086; Thomas Carothers, *In the Name of Democracy: U.S. Policy toward Latin America in the Reagan Years* (Berkeley: University of California Press, 1991); and Howard J. Wiarda, *The Democratic Revolution in Latin America* (New York: A Twentieth Century Fund Book, Holmes and Meier, 1990).

6. See Joshua Muravchik, *The Uncertain Crusade: Jimmy Carter and the Dilemma of Human Rights Policy* (Lanham, Md.: Hamilton Press, 1986).

7. Michael Mandelbaum, "Foreign Policy as Social Work," *Foreign Affairs* 75 (January/February 1996): 16–32; Howard J. Wiarda, ed., *American Foreign and Strategic Policy in the Post-Cold War World* (Westport, Conn.: Greenwood Press, 1996); and Thomas Carothers, "Democracy Promotion under Clinton," *Washington Quarterly* 18 (Autumn 1995): 13–28.

8. Rostow, *The Stages of Economic Growth* (Cambridge, England: Cambridge University Press, 1960).

9. See the collection of articles in the *Journal of Interamerican Studies and World Affairs* 38 (January 1997).

Chapter 2

1. Steve Boilard, *Russia at the Twenty-First Century* (Orlando and Fort Worth: Harcourt Brace, 1997).

2. See the excellent summary in *Wall Street Journal*, July 3, 1996, p. 1.

3. *Washington Post*, December 31, 1995.

4. See the results of the poll by scholar Peter Reddaway in *Peace Watch* (October 1995): 10–11.

5. A. H. Somjee and Geeta Somjee, *Development Success in Asia-Pacific* (New York: St. Martin's, 1995); Raul S. Manglapus, *Will of the People: Original Democracy in Non-Western Societies* (New York: Freedom House, 1987); Harold Lasswell, Daniel Lerner, and John Montgomery, eds., *Values and Development: Appraising Asian Experience* (Cambridge: MIT Press, 1976); Robert A. Scalapino, *The Politics of Development: Perspectives of Twentieth Century Asia* (Cambridge: Harvard University Press, 1989).

6. For example, Sumio Okahashi, "The Myth of Universality: Cultural Differences between the United States and Japan," *Speaking of Japan* 9 (February 1989): 1–4.

7. *The Economist* (May 28, 1994): 13; (January 14, 1995): 13, 19–21; *Wall Street Journal*, April 13, 1994, p. 1ff.

8. Peter R. Moody, Jr., *Tradition and Modernization in China and Japan* (Belmont, Calif.: Wadsworth Publishing, 1995); *The Economist* (January 21, 1995): 38–39.

9. Max Weber, *The Protestant Ethic and the Spirit of Capitalism*, various editions (London: George Allen and Unwin, 1930).

10. Howard J. Wiarda, *Corporatism and Comparative Politics* (New York: M. E. Sharpe, 1996).

11. Kishore Mahbubani, "Asia and a United States in Decline," *Washington Quarterly* 17 (Spring 1994): 5–24.

12. *Washington Post*, April 22, 1994, p. A33; *Wall Street Journal*, April 13, 1994, p. 1ff.

13. See Dale Herspring, "Eastern Europe," in Howard J. Wiarda, ed., *Non-Western Theories of Change* (Orlando and Fort Worth: Harcourt Brace, 1997).

14. The classic study is S. M. Lipset, *Political Man: The Social Bases of Politics*, expanded edition (Baltimore: Johns Hopkins University Press, 1981).

15. See *Wall Street Journal*, August 28, 1996, p. 12; *Washington Post*, September 8, 1996, p. C7; *Washington Post*, October 13, 1996, p. A1; *New York Times*, March 27, 1996, p. 21; *Christian Science Monitor*, June 13, 1996, p. 19; *New York Review of Books*, November 4, 1993.

16. *The Economist* (August 6, 1994), Special Insert, "Islam and the West."

17. Bernard Lewis, *Islam and the West* (New York: Oxford University Press, 1993); Mark Juergensmeyer, *The New Cold War: Religious Nationalism Confronts the Secular State* (Berkeley: University of California Press, 1993).

18. Ozay Mehmet, *Islamic Identity and Development* (London: Routledge, 1990); Leonard Binder, *Islamic Liberalism* (Chicago: University of Chicago Press, 1988); Hamid Enayat, *Modern Islamic Political Thought* (Austin: University of Texas Press, 1982); Mohamed El-Awa, *The Political System of the Islamic State* (Indianapolis: American Trust Publications, 1980).

19. For the strong argument—which, however, ignores the policy's domestic political attractiveness—that a morally based U.S. agenda based on the mistaken notion of congruent universal values is not only parochial but dangerously mistaken and destabilizing in its application, see Adda B. Bozeman, "American Policy and the Illusion of Congruent

Values," *Strategic Review* (Winter 1987): 11–223; also Bozeman's book, *Strategic Intelligence and Statecraft* (New York: Brassey's, 1993).

20. David Apter, *The Gold Coast in Transition* (Princeton: Princeton University Press, 1955); Ruth Schacter Morgenthau, *Political Parties in French-Speaking West Africa* (Oxford, England: Clarendon Press, 1964).

21. Marina Ottaway, "Should Elections Be the Criterion of Democratization in Africa?" *CSIS Africa Notes*, no. 145 (February 1993).

22. "Polls to Nowhere," *The Economist* (November 23, 1996): 20–21; Marina Ottaway, "African Democratization: An Update," *CSIS Africa Notes*, no. 171 (April 1995).

23. Ottaway, "Should Elections Be the Criterion?" 4.

24. I. William Zartman, "Africa in the Year 2000: Some Key Political Variables," *CSIS Africa Notes*, no. 161 (June 1994).

25. Lana Wylie, "Sub-Saharan Africa: Western Influence and Indigenous Realities," in Wiarda, ed., *Non-Western*; Ali Mazrui, *The Africans: A Triple Heritage* (London: BBC Publications, 1986); Claude Ake, *Democracy and Development in Africa* (Washington, D.C.: Brookings Institution, 1996); Naomi Chazan, ed., *Politics and Society in Contemporary Africa* (Boulder, Colo.: Lynne Rienner, 1992).

Chapter 3

1. See Howard J. Wiarda, ed., *The Continuing Struggle for Democracy in Latin America* (Boulder, Colo.: Westview Press, 1977).

2. The more optimistic update is presented in my book, *Latin American Politics: A New World of Possibilities* (Belmont, Calif.: Wadsworth Publishers, 1994).

3. See the special issue devoted to these themes of the *Journal of Interamerican Studies and World Affairs*, January 1997.

4. See, among many sources, Riordan Roett, ed., *Political and Economic Liberalization in Mexico* (Boulder: Lynne Rienner, 1993); M. Delal Baer and Sidney Weintraub, eds., *The NAFTA Debate* (Boulder: Lynne Rienner, 1994); Howard J. Wiarda, "Mexico: The Unraveling of a Corporatist Regime," *Journal of Interamerican Studies and World Affairs* 30 (Winter 1988–1989); and Charles F. Doran and Alvin Paul Drischler, eds., *A New North America: Cooperation and Enhanced Interdependence* (Westport, Conn.: Praeger, 1996).

5. The best studies are those by Georges A. Fairiol and his collaborators, *The Haitian Challenge* (Washington, D.C.: Center for Strategic

and International Studies, 1993); *Haitian Frustration: Dilemmas of U.S. Policy* (Washington, D.C.: CSIS, 1995); and Ernest H. Preeg, *The Haitian Dilemma* (Washington, D.C.: CSIS, 1995).

6. Lipset, *Political Man*.

7. Tocqueville, *Democracy in America*, many editions.

8. Maguire, "The Grassroots Movement," in Fauriol, ed., *Haitian Frustrations*, 145–150.

9. Preeg, *Haitian Dilemma*.

10. Talbott, "Spreading Democracy," *Foreign Affairs* 75 (November/December 1996): 47–63.

11. The case against Aristide's "democratic" credentials has been made by Elliott Abrams, "Haiti: Playing Out the Options," in Fauriol, ed., *Haitian Frustrations*, 69–74.

12. See the analysis of David Scott Palmer, "Peru: The Enduring Authoritarian Legacy," in Howard J. Wiarda and Harvey F. Kline, eds., *Latin American Politics and Development*, 4th ed. (Boulder: Westview Press, 1996), 200–226.

13. David Scott Palmer, ed., *Shining Path of Peru* (New York: St. Martin's, 1996).

14. For the background see Roland Ebel, "Guatemala: Politics in a Central American City-State," in Wiarda and Kline, eds., *Latin American Politics*, 453–474.

15. John D. Martz and David J. Myers, *Venezuela: The Democratic Experience* (Westport, Conn.: Greenwood Press, 1986; Iêda Siqueira Wiarda, "Venezuela: The Politics of Democratic Development," in Wiarda and Kline, eds., *Latin American Politics*, 3rd ed. (1985).

16. Luis J. Oropeza, *Tutelary Pluralism: A Critical Approach to Venezuelan Democracy* (Cambridge, Mass.: Center for International Affairs, Harvard University, 1983).

17. Anibal Romero, *Decadencia y Crisis de la Democracia* (Caracas: Ed. Panapo, 1994).

18. *Cultura democrática en Venezuela* (Caracas: Consultores 21, 1996).

19. For background, Howard J. Wiarda and Michael J. Kryzanek, *The Dominican Republic: Caribbean Crucible*, 2nd ed. (Boulder: Westview Press, 1992).

20. Howard J. Wiarda, "The 1996 Dominican Republic Election" (Washington, D.C.: CSIS Western Hemisphere Election Study Series, 1996).

21. Isis Duarte et al., *Cultura Política y Democracia en República*

Dominicana (Santo Domingo: Pontifical Catholic University Madre y Maestra, 1996).

Chapter 4

1. *Freedom House News* (December 18, 1996): 1ff.; *Freedom Review* (January-February 1997).
2. For a general treatment of Third World trends, see Howard J. Wiarda, *Ethnocentrism in Foreign Policy: Can We Understand the Third World?* (Washington, D.C.: American Enterprise Institute, 1983).
3. Conversation with the author and others, at U.S. Department of State briefing on Venezuela, 1994.
4. See my book, *American Foreign Policy: Actors and Processes* (New York: Harper Collins, 1996).
5. Don Piper and Ronald Terchak, eds., *Interaction: Foreign Policy and Public Policy* (Washington, D.C.: American Enterprise Institute, 1983).

Select Bibliography

Abrams, Elliott. "Haiti: Playing Out the Options." In Georges A. Fauriol, ed. *Haitian Frustrations: Dilemmas for U.S. Policy*. Washington, D.C.: Center for Strategic and International Studies, 1995, 69-74.

Ake, Claude. *Democracy and Development in Africa*. Washington, D.C.: Brookings Institution, 1996.

Apter, David. *The Gold Coast in Transition*. Princeton: Princeton University Press, 1955.

Baer, M. Delal, and Sidney Weintraub, eds. *The NAFTA Debate*. Boulder, Colo.: Lynne Rienner, 1994.

Bernstein, Carl, and Marco Politi. *His Holiness: John Paul II and the Hidden History of Our Time*. New York: Doubleday, 1996.

Binder, Leonard. *Islamic Liberalism*. Chicago: University of Chicago Press, 1988.

Boilard, Steve. *Russia at the Twenty-First Century*. Orlando and Fort Worth: Harcourt Brace, 1997.

Bozeman, Adda B. "American Policy and the Illusion of Congruent Values." *Strategic Review* (Winter 1987): 11-223.

_____. *Strategic Intelligence and Statecraft*. New York: Brassey's, 1993.

Carothers, Thomas. "Democracy Promotion under Clinton." *Washington Quarterly* 18 (Autumn 1995): 13-28.

_____. *In the Name of Democracy: U.S. Policy toward Latin America in the Reagan Years*. Berkeley: University of California Press, 1991.

Chazan, Naomi, ed. *Politics and Society in Contemporary Africa*. Boulder, Colo.: Lynne Rienner, 1992.

Cultura democrática en Venezuela. Caracas: Consultores 21, 1996.

Diamond, Larry. *Promoting Democracy in the 1990s*. Washington, D.C.: Carnegie Commission, 1995.

Doran, Charles F., and Alvin Paul Drischler, eds. *A New North America: Cooperation and Enhanced Interdependence*. Westport, Conn.: Praeger, 1996.

Duarte, Isis, et al. *Cultura Política y Democracia en República Dominicana*. Santo Domingo: Pontifical Catholic University Madre y Maestra, 1996.

Ebel, Roland. "Guatemala: Politics in a Central American City-State." In Wiarda and Kline, eds., *Latin American Politics and Development*, 453-474.

El-Awa, Mohamed S. *On the Political System of the Islamic State*. Indianapolis: American Trust Publications, 1980.

Enayat, Hamid. *Modern Islamic Political Thought*. Austin: University of Texas Press, 1982.

Fauriol, Georges A., ed. *The Haitian Challenge*. Washington, D.C.: Center for Strategic and International Studies, 1993.

_____, ed. *Haitian Frustrations: Dilemmas for U.S. Policy*. Washington, D.C.: Center for Strategic and International Studies, 1995.

Freedom House News (December 18, 1996): 1ff.; *Freedom Review* (January-February 1997).

Hartz, Louis. *The Liberal Tradition in America*. New York: Harcourt Brace, 1955.

Herspring, Dale. "Eastern Europe." In Wiarda, ed., *Non-Western Theories of Change*.

Huntington, Samuel P. *The Clash of Civilizations and the Remaking of World Order*. New York: Simon and Schuster, 1996.

_____. *The Third Wave: Democratization in the Late Twentieth Century*. Norman: University of Oklahoma Press, 1991.

Jacoby, Tamar. "The Reagan Turnabout on Human Rights." *Foreign Affairs* (Summer 1986): 1066-1086.

Juergensmeyer, Mark. *The New Cold War: Religious Nationalism Confronts the Secular State*. Berkeley: University of California Press, 1993.

Lasswell, Harold, Daniel Lerner, and John Montgomery, eds. *Values and Development: Appraising Asian Experience*. Cambridge: MIT Press, 1976.

Lewis, Bernard. *Islam and the West*. New York: Oxford University Press, 1993.

Lipset, S.M. *American Exceptionalism: A Double-Edged Sword*. New York: W. W. Norton, 1996.

_____. *Political Man: The Social Bases of Politics*. Expanded edition. Baltimore: Johns Hopkins University Press, 1981.

Lowenthal, Abraham F., ed. *Exporting Democracy: The United States and Latin America*. Baltimore: Johns Hopkins University Press, 1991.

Maguire, Robert. "The Grassroots Movement." In Fauriol, ed., *Haitian Frustrations*, 145-150.

Mahbubani, Kishore. "Asia and a United States in Decline." *Washington Quarterly* 17 (Spring 1994): 5-24.

Mandelbaum, Michael. "Foreign Policy as Social Work." *Foreign Affairs* 75 (January/February 1996): 16-32.

Manglapus, Raul S. *Will of the People: Original Democracy in Non-Western Societies*. New York: Freedom House, 1987.

Martz, John D., and David J. Myers. *Venezuela: The Democratic Experience*. Westport, Conn.: Greenwood Press, 1986.

Mazrui, Ali. *The Africans: A Triple Heritage*. London: BBC Publications, 1986.

Mehmet, Ozay. *Islamic Identity and Development*. London: Routledge, 1990.

Moody, Peter R., Jr. *Tradition and Modernization in China and Japan*. Belmont, Calif.: Wadsworth Publishing, 1995.

Morgenthau, Ruth Schacter. *Political Parties in French-Speaking West Africa*. Oxford, England: Clarendon Press, 1964.

Muravchik, Joshua. *Exporting Democracy: Fulfilling America's Destiny*. Washington, D.C.: AEI Press, 1991.

_____. *The Uncertain Crusade: Jimmy Carter and the Dilemma of Human Rights Policy*. Lanham, Md.: Hamilton Press, 1986.

Okahashi, Sumio. "The Myth of Universality: Cultural Differences between the United States and Japan." *Speaking of Japan* 9 (February 1989): 1-4.

Oropeza, Luis J. *Tutelary Pluralism: A Critical Approach to Venezuelan Democracy*. Cambridge, Mass.: Center for International Affairs, Harvard University, 1983.

Ottaway, Marina. "African Democratization: An Update." *CSIS Africa Notes*, no. 171 (April 1995).

_____. "Should Elections Be the Criterion of Democratization in Africa?" *CSIS Africa Notes*, no. 145 (February 1993).

Palmer, David Scott. "Peru: The Enduring Authoritarian Legacy." In Wiarda and Kline, eds. *Latin American Politics and Development*, 200-226.

_____, ed. *Shining Path of Peru*. New York: St. Martin's, 1996.

Piper, Don, and Ronald Terchak, eds., *Interaction: Foreign Policy and*

Public Policy. Washington, D.C.: American Enterprise Institute, 1983.

Pipes, Daniel, and Adam Garfinkle, eds. *Friendly Tyrants: An American Dilemma*. New York: Doubleday, 1991.

Preeg, Ernest H. *The Haitian Dilemma*. Washington, D.C.: CSIS, 1995.

Report of the President's National Bipartisan Commission on Central America. New York: Macmillan, 1984.

Roett, Riordan, ed. *Political and Economic Liberalization in Mexico*. Boulder, Colo.: Lynne Rienner, 1993.

Romero, Anibal. *Decadencia y Crisis de la Democracía*. Caracas: Ed. Panapo, 1994.

Rostow, W.W. *The Stages of Economic Growth*. Cambridge, England: Cambridge University Press, 1960.

Scalapino, Robert A. *The Politics of Development: Perspectives of Twentieth Century Asia*. Cambridge: Harvard University Press, 1989.

Smith, Tony. *America's Mission: The United States and the Worldwide Struggle for Democracy in the Twentieth Century*. Princeton, N.J.: Princeton University Press, 1994.

Somjee, A.H., and Geeta Somjee. *Development Success in Asia-Pacific*. New York: St. Martin's, 1995.

Talbott, Strobe. "Spreading Democracy." *Foreign Affairs* 75 (November/December 1996): 47-63.

Tocqueville, Alexis de. *Democracy in America*. Many editions.

Weber, Max. *The Protestant Ethic and the Spirit of Capitalism*. Various editions. London: George Allen and Unwin, 1930.

Wiarda, Howard J. *American Foreign Policy: Actors and Processes*. New York: Harper Collins, 1996.

_____. "Can Democracy Be Exported? The Quest for Democracy in U.S. Latin America Policy." Occasional Paper No. 157. Washington, D.C.: Woodrow Wilson International Center for Scholars, Smithsonian Institution. Reprinted in Kevin Middlebrook and Carlos Rico, eds. *The United States and Latin America*. Pittsburgh: University of Pittsburgh Press, 1985.

_____. "Consensus Found, Consensus Lost: Disjunctures in U.S. Policy toward Latin America at the Turn of the Century." *Journal of Interamerican Studies and World Affairs* 39 (Spring 1997): 13-31.

_____. *Corporatism and Comparative Politics*. New York: M. E. Sharpe, 1996.

_____. *The Democratic Revolution in Latin America*. New York: Twentieth Century Fund Book, Holmes and Meier, 1990.

_____. "The 1996 Dominican Republic Election." Washington, D.C.: CSIS Western Hemisphere Election Study Series, 1996.

_____. *Ethnocentrism in Foreign Policy: Can We Understand the Third World?* Washington, D.C.: American Enterprise Institute, 1983.

_____. *Latin American Politics: A New World of Possibilities*. Belmont, Calif.: Wadsworth Publishers, 1994.

_____. "Mexico: The Unraveling of a Corporatist Regime." *Journal of Interamerican Studies and World Affairs* 30 (Winter 1988-1989).

_____. "U.S. Policy and Democracy in the Caribbean and Latin America." CSIS Policy Papers on the Americas. Washington, D.C.: CSIS, 1995.

Wiarda, Howard J., ed. *American Foreign and Strategic Policy in the Post-Cold War World*. Westport, Conn.: Greenwood Press, 1996.

_____, ed. *The Continuing Struggle for Democracy in Latin America*. Boulder, Colo.: Westview Press, 1977.

_____, ed. *Non-Western Theories of Change*. Orlando and Fort Worth: Harcourt Brace, 1997.

Wiarda, Howard J., and Harvey Kline, eds. *Latin American Politics and Development*. 4th edition. Boulder, Colo.: Westview Press, 1996.

Wiarda, Howard J., and Michael J. Kryzanek. *The Dominican Republic: Caribbean Crucible*. 2nd edition. Boulder: Westview Press, 1992.

Wiarda, Iêda Siqueira. "Venezuela: The Politics of Democratic Development." In Wiarda and Kline, eds. *Latin American Politics and Development*.

Wylie, Lana. "Sub-Saharan Africa: Western Influence and Indigenous Realities." In Wiarda, ed., *Non-Western Theories of Change*.

Zartman, I. William. "Africa in the Year 2000: Some Key Political Variables." *CSIS Africa Notes*, no. 161 (June 1994).

Index

Africa: political and economic development, 42–48; U.S. policy toward, 41–43
Agency for International Development (USAID): Democracy Office, 43; in Dominican Republic (1994), 74
Albania, 32
Albright, Madeleine, 12
Algeria, 40
Alliance for Progress, 10, 49
Aristide, Jean Bertrand, 59–62, 73
Authoritarianism: Africa, 42, 45; Confucianism as justification for, 28–29; continuum in transition to democracy, 77, 80–81; Czech Republic, 33; Dominican Republic, 71–72; East Asian nations, 27–31; Fujimori's regime in Peru, 63–64; in Islamic countries, 37–41; Latin America, 49–50; Mexico, 52–53, 55–56; post-Soviet Russia, 26; Russia, 23; Serrano's regime in Guatemala, 65–66

Balaguer, Joaquín, 71–74
Bosnia: political, economic, and social problems of, 35; U.S. foreign policy in, 35–37, 83

Brzezinski, Zbigniew, 54–55
Bulgaria: economic and political problems of, 34; as emerging Eastern European country, 32
Bush administration: foreign policy, 11–12; justification for Persian Gulf intervention, 2–3; realistic-idealistic mix in foreign policy, 82

Caldera, Rafael, 69–70
Carter administration: foreign policy and human rights agenda, 10–11, 13, 49; idealistic foreign policy, 6, 82
China: human rights in, 7–8, 79; MFN status, 7–8, 78, 87; political and economic development, 30–31
Christopher, Warren, 11–12, 82
Clergy and Laity Concerned, 14
Clinton administration: human rights focus of foreign policy, 12; intervention in Haiti, 60–61, 81; opposition to Balaguer in Dominican Republic (1994), 73; retreaded Carter foreign policy, 12, 82–83; trend from romanticism to idealistic-realistic, 82–83; use of interaction of domestic and foreign policy, 85

101

About the Author

Howard J. Wiarda is Professor of Foreign Policy and Political Science and holds the Leonard J. Horwitz Chair of Latin American and Iberian Studies at the University of Massachusetts/Amherst. He is also Senior Associate of the Center for Strategic and International Studies. Professor Wiarda has published extensively on foreign and strategic policy issues, comparative politics, the developing nations, Southern Europe, Latin America, and East Asia. His more recent books include *American Foreign Policy: Actors and Processes*, *Democracy and Its Discontents*, *U.S. Foreign and Strategic Policy in the Post-Cold War Era*, *Introduction to Comparative Politics*, *Latin American Politics and Development*, and *Politics in Iberia*. He serves as an adviser and consultant to the Department of State, the Department of Defense, and other government agencies and private businesses.